WHICH ONE OF YOU IS
Copyright 2015 by Sean M

CW00422066

Acknowledgements

To everyone who has supported us on this adoption journey, thank you for celebrating and embracing a new kind of family. We are also grateful to all those who worked behind the scenes to bring our family together, especially Cristina Williams and Brandi and Neal Plaster in Oregon, and Beth Anderson, Erica Gump, Cathy Nogay, and Rhonda Stubbs in West Virginia. And lastly thank you to everyone at Three Rivers Adoption Council, most notably Kristen Matthews, Kelly Sagel, Beth Carson, Nikki Kazarick, Debbie Taylor, Chenelle Brown and Chenlin Lao.

To Chris, Elijah and Todd
Everything and Always

Love, Dad

Table of Contents

The Ending (or, The Prologue) 4

Which One of You Is the Mother? 7

The Future Is Now 14

Adoption for Dummies 19

Through the Looking Glass 28

My Two Dads 33

This Ain't Shakespeare, Kid 41

Eye of the Tiger 48

The Story of Us 55

No More Goodbyes 64

Crying on the Toilet & Other Bathroom Distractions 70

Gladys Kravitz Doesn't Live Here Anymore 77

Sometimes I'm Fat 84

That's What Friends Are For 91

Be Careful What You Google 97

The Name Game 103

How to Survive the Holidays 111

The Last Days of Disco 119

The Beginning (or, The Epilogue) 126

THE ENDING (OR, THE PROLOGUE)

On each of the forms I cross out *Mother* and write in *Father*. I do this at the doctor's office and the adoption agency, and on permission slips throughout the school year. I do this not because I am trying to make a point or engage in an act of passive protest or even because I am offended. I do this because this is who we are: we are two men raising two children.

We are not the first people to do this.

We are not breaking down barriers.

We are not role models.

We are just a family.

We stand out by being extraordinarily ordinary. We lead by example. No bells and whistles, no banners or flags, no begging everyone else to like and accept us as if our worth could only be measured by the number of people who validate our life choices or like our latest Facebook posts. Our approval is not measured in retweets or number of followers. And while we may flood social media with photos of our family and share anecdotal stories about our children in blog posts, those are just snapshots in time; nothing more than the highlight reel from a "best of" episode of a long-running TV series.

We may be two men raising two children but the truth is without the edits we would be Must-Flee TV. Who wants to watch two middle-aged men grocery shopping? Or sitting around the dining room table paying bills? Or arguing over the right way to fold socks while their kids argue over who gets to be first player in *MarioKart*? I doubt even TLC has an audience willing to watch me watch *Law & Order* reruns five nights a week.

I don't like to think of us as boring, just profoundly unremarkable.

We may have been interesting once upon a time, engaging in our fair share of debauchery, but that was *before we had kids*. We were in our twenties; debauchery is expected of one in their twenties. But then you turn thirty and being debauched seems like too much work and now that we're in our forties it just feels desperate. Also, we're just too tired.

We've traded in our leather chaps for mom jeans.

Now every morning my husband makes breakfast and every night I cook dinner and in between we tend to the kids. We live our lives openly in plain sight. We cross out *Mother* and write in *Father*. We are two men raising two children. We are just a family.

WHICH ONE OF YOU IS THE MOTHER?

Recently a well-meaning idiot said to me, "You're such a good person." This was in reference to learning that I had adopted my children. As if the simple act of adopting a child had cosmically voided the very long list of not so nice things I've done in my life, transforming me overnight into a saint. I am not a saint. I once made someone cry and enjoyed it. I am currently holding grudges that date back to the Reagan administration. When people ask me for spare change/a moment of my time/help performing the Heimlich maneuver, I roll my eyes. It's not that I don't have compassion, I do. I just don't give it away like a twink with daddy issues at a bear bar.

And I have tried to change. I have tried to be a different person. But the truth for all of us, I believe, is you will never stop being the person you are. Like a recovering addict in a twelve-step program, the best I can hope to do is resist temptation. And now that I'm a parent I need to lead by example. I need to toss my spare change into the cup. I need to forgive. I need to stop making people cry, and if I do, I at least need to stop enjoying it so much.

At the end of the day the world has enough people in it like me: cynics who laugh at those gullible chumps tearfully posting three-legged dog videos on Facebook before dumping ice on their heads and then declaring in a recycled meme "I will not be defined by my past". Just because I'm a (middle-aged) mean girl doesn't mean my children have to be too.

You're such a good person. It's a judgment dripping with condescension, the subtext screaming, "Poor unwanted orphans saved from a life in the workhouses." This isn't nineteenth century France. This isn't *Les Miserables*. I am not Jean Valjean.

You're such a good person. It's a sentiment on par with, "He looks just like you." It's a lie people feel compelled to tell. *He looks just like you.* Yes, my skinny long-limbed five-foot three-inch tall nine year old with high cheekbones and Native American ancestry looks just like my short-waisted stout full-faced pasty white Irish ass. At least when people say it to my husband I think, "Well, they do both wear glasses". I know people are just being nice, just reading from the script, but still, it does make me wonder what people would say if we had adopted a black kid. *He looks just like you. But darker.*

The observation doesn't offend me; it amuses me. *He looks just like you.* It makes me feel like I'm part of the club. The first thing we say to new parents when presented with their baby is, "He looks just like you!" It's written into the script. Except adoption flips the script and that makes people uncomfortable and when people are uncomfortable they say stupid things. They overcompensate. They say the words they think we want to hear as if we had walked into the adoption agency and said, "I'll take a seven year old, but make sure he looks just like us. We don't want people getting any funny ideas."

He looks just like you.

It's a twentieth century trope harkening back to the not-so glory days of adoption. Black babies with black families. Italian babies with Italian families. Gay babies with gay families. (I'm totally joking about that last example. Everyone knows you aren't born gay.) Just two generations ago every attempt was made to bury the adoption, to keep the secret. Children grew up being lied to; their origin a shame so catastrophic its revelation would destroy a family, becoming fodder for yet another C-grade *Lifetime* movie of the week.

Now in these early days of the twenty-first century we celebrate adoption in all its forms. Adoption is chic. It even has the high holy Brangelina seal of approval. Today families of all shapes and sizes and colors openly parade around like some 1984 Benetton ad. Two years ago when we adopted our first son, we found ourselves joining the ranks of all those Benetton families that came before us. By simple virtue of being gay men with a camera-ready minority child straight out of central boy band casting we were all the rage.

People were incredibly supportive. Friends sent cards and gifts. Co-workers offered heartfelt congratulations and encouragement. Strangers in restaurants met our eyes with enthusiastic *You-go-girl!* grins. Everyone seemed to be genuinely happy for our happiness in a way that went beyond the specifics of our situation. They didn't see two gay guys and a couple of kids, they saw a family. Ultimately our big gay adoption was a non-event and I liked that because it meant we were living in a time and place where something as superficial as our sexuality was irrelevant.

And for the most part that has remained true. But every now and again I am met with this question: *Which one of you is the mother?* The first time someone asked me that question I laughed, thinking it was a joke. But when she repeated it and I realized she was serious, I was just confused. I mean, honestly, how in the hell do you answer that question?

"Which one of you is the mother?" Well, if we're talking in strict biological terms then the answer is neither of us because we're both dudes which means we have guy parts in our downstairs.

"Which one of you is the mother?" Well, if we're *not* talking in strict biological terms then we must be relying on gender stereotypes; therefore, as the more emotional of the two, I suppose that I fit the maternal role. But then in terms of household duties it's a 50/50 split: I clean, but my husband does the laundry, and we both do the cooking. My husband is better at dressing cuts and bruises, whereas I just look better in a dress. And while he delivers award-winning hugs, I am just plain award-winning in my impersonation of Faye Dunaway as Joan Crawford screaming, "Tina, bring me the axe!"

Ultimately the problem with the question is that it is not *the* question. They ask, "Which one of you is the mother?" but what they really mean to say is, "Which one of you is the *woman?*" It's that age-old heterosexual preoccupation the straights have with two guys and sex: what goes where? It's such an odd fascination. I never look at a heterosexual couple and think, "I wonder where he puts his penis". (In her ear. It goes in her ear, right?) Straight men feel the need to feminize gay men, but let me tell you there is nothing girly about taking one in the fanny. It's that simple.

Which one of you is the mother? Perhaps the question is a test. An opportunity for the naysayers to check under the hood, a vagina being the golden ticket to legitimacy. Everyone knows a child raised by two men is unnatural, a recruiting tactic for a sinister endgame: GAY WORLD DOMINATION. The powers that be can't further risk the whole of the heterosexual empire being toppled by an army of show-tune-singing leather-onesie-wearing babies in Cher wigs.

Which one of you is the mother? I don't know why people ask it. I suppose it's irrelevant. Still, I hate that question and I hate that anyone even considers it when they see my family. But some people cannot see beyond the confines of their shallow imaginations and narrow experiences. I suppose two guys breaking God's law makes for better TV than two guys driving their kids to school. As for which one of us is the woman, I can't say for sure. Everyone knows once you've been together for almost twenty years *nothing* goes *anywhere*. Frankly, now that we have two kids I have neither the time nor the energy to put anything anywhere. Of course when something does go somewhere we do it just like everyone else, but gayer. Much gayer.

THE FUTURE IS NOW

Two years ago my husband and I decided to start a family. With no viable means to house a tiny pre-human for nine months due to the lack of a decent functioning uterus between us -- we're both men, you remember -- we made the decision to adopt. Or rather, it made us. At that point in our relationship we had been together for sixteen years so it was get another dog, adopt a kid or grow old in a suffocating air of quiet mutual resentment. Two kids and one dog later and we are in deep. Our once-spotless hardwood floors are now covered by a carpet of forgotten toys. We eat chicken nuggets for breakfast and pancakes for dinner. *We own a minivan.*

Looking back I can't remember what our lives were like before the boys agreed to let us be their dads. We had friends, we had jobs, we had hobbies. I know we had a life before our children, but in retrospect, I think we were just killing time until we could adopt them.

The day we became parents our lives changed. Parenthood rewrote our story. It gave us an ending that honored our beginning. On the first anniversary of my oldest son's adoption I wrote this in a card: *Something that is meant to happen is called fate. It is decided from before the beginning. You were our fate. You were born to be our son.*

I had wanted to be a Dad for as long as I could remember. Having a family was my future. When I was younger I imagined a family photo that included a very understanding wife and our six smiling children. As I grew older and came to realize that I was gay, the photo changed. I still pictured the six smiling kids, but my once-very understanding wife was now a hot guy named Juan. In the end I got my guy and, while he may have lacked the ethnic flair of a Juan, we built a perfectly imperfect life together.

We first met eighteen years ago. I was working at a small grocery store in my hometown. My would-be boyfriend/future husband lived across the street. I remember the first time I saw Todd he came in to buy bleach and toothpaste, an intriguing combination. It was cold outside that first day that I saw him and he was wearing a knit cap; he looked adorable and lost and the minute he put that cap on his head I knew I loved him. Or at the very least, liked him more than donuts. It was that simple.

Todd came into the store several times throughout the week. Eventually I worked up the courage to ask him out, this future father of my children. Like any self-respecting homosexual man masquerading as a giggling teenage schoolgirl I slipped a handwritten note into his grocery bag. *Would you like to go out with me?* The only thing missing were the two boxes for him to indicate either *yes* or *no*.

We took a lot of walks in those first few weeks, each evening stroll capped off by an awkward side hug. It was all very chaste and puritanical. I began to worry he wasn't gay the night I leaned in to kiss him and he turned his cheek. I was mortified to think I had misread the situation, but I also really enjoyed spending time with him. So I checked my embarrassment at the door and we continued our evening walks. A few nights later he did not turn his cheek.

We were never a perfect match. From our first kiss on that cold snowy February night, we were always just slightly out-of-step. He wouldn't talk enough and I would talk too much. I'd kick back with a bottle of cold beer while he'd unwind with a cup of hot tea. I wanted more when he had enough. We brought out the best in each other by acknowledging the worst. We were perfectly mismatched.

Over the years Todd has forgiven so much — my lack of patience, my tendency to overreact, my ability to make everything about me. In return for looking past this catalog of flaws and shortcomings, I forgive him for taking too long to tell a story and not being named Juan. Eighteen years later and there is no one I would rather share uncomfortable silences with than him.

We talked about starting a family very early in our relationship, the two of us mapping out our future in that impossibly tiny single bed in my first apartment. It was something we both wanted. We discussed having children at length, revisiting the idea often throughout the years. But there always seemed to be a reason not to move forward. We were struggling financially. We had just moved to a new city. We weren't ready to be parents.

But still, the idea remained. No matter what our situation it seemed to always be there – hanging over us just slightly out of reach because, really, who would give two gay guys a kid? And so as the years passed we talked about it less and less. We occupied ourselves with other distractions. We created new dreams to forget the old.

Life went on.

A dozen years into our relationship and I asked my still-not-yet-but-someday-soon-husband if we were ever going to have a family and he said, "No, it just isn't going to happen." It was devastating to hear and I was angry with him for saying it, but then I realized he said it for the same reason we had done nothing more than *imagine* the idea: FEAR. We had talked and dreamed and schemed but we had never taken any real action. In all those years, we had done nothing more than float the idea of having children as if the idea alone would make our dream a reality.

So one day we did something.

There was an adoption agency a few blocks from where I worked. I called and made an appointment for us to meet with an adoption specialist. One week later on August 7, 2012, Todd and I walked through the doors of the adoption agency and into our future.

ADOPTION FOR DUMMIES

Adoption is easy. I don't care what you've heard to the contrary because it's not true. *Adoption is easy.* Yes, there are hundreds of pages of paperwork to fill out, and yes, your privacy will be invaded, and yes, the process will seem never-ending, and yes, there will be days of rejection that crush your soul where you feel absolutely inadequate and lose all hope. But I like having my soul crushed and I enjoy being made to feel inadequate; it makes me want it more. And I didn't mind the mountains of paperwork or the scores of invasive questions; it brought Todd and me closer together. Adoption is easy.

You have to do the work, but the work is worth the doing. So you fill out a few hundred papers, so you answer a couple thousand questions, so you wait the better part of a year, who cares? Because in the end someone gives you a kid.

Adoption is easy. It will steal your time. It will require your patience. It will demand your honesty.

You just need to be honest with yourself about what you can handle from a child. As we filled out the paperwork I could hear the voice of the adoption resource supervisor echoing in my head. Her name was NeNe. Her hair was on-point and she had sass for days. It was August 7, 2012. We had just walked into the adoption agency. After 15 years of talking about starting a family we were finally doing it. NeNe was the first person we met at the agency. Over the course of the next several months we heard her words repeated back to us by a series of case managers, matching specialists, and a woman named Jennifer who taught our parenting classes.

The classes were intense. We were holed up in a conference room with a dozen other would-be parents for eight hours every Saturday for six weeks. We sat around a large table, each of us flanked by mountains of unfinished paperwork, watching a series of poorly lit videos and listening to cautionary tales of adoptions gone wrong. Everyone in the videos was an expert and they all spoke in low soothing tones because as experts they expected us to speak to our future children in low soothing tones. (I employed this technique for about a week, which is coincidentally also how long before I said, "Screw it!" and drank a beer in front of my kid.) No matter what the situation as parents we were instructed never to raise our voices above a hushed whisper. *You set the dog on fire? I think someone needs some redirection. But first let's start with a hug.*

I came to dislike these experts and their hug-it-out psychology. I found myself mentally retreating to the shadows of their poorly lit close-ups, biding my time until the moment I could hug every last gasp of self-important pomposity out of them. They were smug know-it-alls, which I suppose is the very definition of being an expert, but still they bothered me. Also, their voices put me to sleep and that's the story of how I learned to nap with my eyes open.

The cautionary tales and case studies were far more interesting and provoked thoughtful discussions among the class. These discussions emphasized the importance of knowing your limits and the necessity of being prepared to live with your decisions. The students in our class ran the gamut from a woman so desperate to be a mother she had cast her net far and wide, declaring there was nothing she could not handle, to the young couple so particular they would settle for nothing less than three boys under the age of five who looked just like them. We all seemed to want a perfect child, except there was no perfect child.

You are not going to get a perfect child.

Many of the children in foster care have been through unimaginable horrors. Jennifer shared several disturbing cases that left me feeling physically sick and emotionally violated. After hearing a particularly obscene story I joked to Todd about needing a series of Meryl Streep *Silkwood* showers in order to feel clean again. I wasn't making light of the story; I had to laugh because if I didn't laugh I would cry. Some of these kids were so broken I couldn't imagine how it was they could ever be put back together.

But that was the point of the class: to prepare you.

Be honest. Don't judge yourself. Don't feel guilty. It was their mantra. Everyone at the agency reminded us that our first responsibility was to meet the needs of our future child and in order to do that we would need to be honest with ourselves. Every child had a different set of needs, some routine and others more complex. We had to be certain that we could meet the required demands.

I read through the exhaustive list of needs and began to tick off the boxes. The more honest I was about what I could handle the more I judged myself. And the more I judged myself the guiltier I felt. These kids had already been through so much and here I was dismissing them because they were in the habit of smearing feces on the wall.

Every child deserves a home, but I was obviously not equipped to give a home to every child. The form was divided into two columns; one side was labeled *Will Consider* and the other side *Unacceptable*. I quickly came to resent the word unacceptable. Every time I checked a condition as unacceptable I felt like I had just pushed an old woman down the stairs. *Starts fires.* Unacceptable. *Tortures animals.* Unacceptable.

I reminded myself there were capable trained families in the foster system that possessed the skills required for children who set fires or injured animals. These families had years of experience and were trained in cases of extreme trauma and emotional disturbance. I told myself those families were real, they existed, but still it was hard to imagine the family that would open their home to a budding arsonist or future serial killer.

Sometimes I would check unacceptable and the reasons were logistical. We lived in an older two-story house with one bathroom on the second floor; we were not equipped to care for a child in a wheelchair. Neither of us knew sign language; we were unable to effectively communicate with a child who was profoundly deaf. One of the categories was "terminal illness". Every child deserves a home, but I'm just not that strong. I can't watch a child die. Can I?

Be honest. Don't feel guilty.

There were categories of mental retardation and then within those categories degrees of challenge. Depression, anxiety, schizophrenia, bipolar disorder. The section ominously titled "medically fragile". There were diseases that were death sentences. There were disorders and conditions that made my breath catch.

I recognize that when you have a child biologically you are not afforded the luxury of choice. Your child is born and he is perfect, even if he isn't. You love him because you do. I won't pretend to know what it is like to love a child who you know will never grow to be an adult. I won't pretend to possess the skills required to care for a child with severe mental challenges. I won't pretend to have answered the form honestly because, like all parents, I don't know what I can handle until the moment I need to handle it.

I think to myself, I just want a child that is healthy. But then, don't we all?

The next series of forms dealt with behavioral needs and something called "special considerations". I discovered that I had no trouble with lying and profanity, but chronic temper tantrums and destructiveness were deal breakers. We also gave a thumbs-down to "sexually acts out" and "excessive masturbation". Doesn't one cancel out the other? I thought to myself.

Excessive masturbation appeared on many forms and each time I saw it I would laugh out loud until the day in class when I learned the reasons behind this behavior. Most often the disorders and behaviors displayed by these kids are manifestations of the horrors they have endured. It says a lot when the least traumatic event in a three year old's life is being taken from his home.

There were many categories we ticked *Will Consider.* We were ready to take on a child with multiple placement history, past adoption disruptions, mild mental retardation, gender identity issues, HIV/AIDS, autism. Children who had been neglected and abused, emotionally and physically. LGBT youth. We were asked about the background of the birth parents and agreed that (with a few exceptions) the sins of the father should not be visited upon the child.

Be honest. Don't judge yourself. Don't feel guilty.

We had to write a personal biography. I spoke about my family and what I had perceived to be a reluctance on their part to support our decision to adopt. I recalled an incident with my parents where they chastised me for not consulting with them before moving forward with the adoption. (Oddly, I don't recall my sister needing to get permission from my parents before getting knocked up.) I wrote about my relationship with Todd. I spoke honestly, describing a difficult period in our relationship where I feared we might not make it. The entire exercise was invasive. It felt unnatural to write so publicly about my private life. But then I remembered that this exercise was designed to match us with the right child; it was testing compatibility. A difficult experience from my past could be the common thread that united me with my future child. So I surrendered my privacy and I told the truth because I knew that truth would help us to realize our dream. I knew the truth would give us our child.

And so it continued. More paperwork, more clearances, more questions, more home visits by well-meaning social workers, more rejection, more waiting.

The only downside to our adoption journey was the waiting. It was the waiting that almost did us in. But here's the truth: the waiting is only bad when you are actually waiting. Yes, days seem like months and weeks feel like years, but from start to finish it really didn't take *that* long. We walked into the adoption agency on August 7, 2012, and three months later we were certified as viable adoptive parents. On April 19, 2013, we read our oldest son's profile for the first time. Five weeks later the state of Oregon approved us as his foster parents and finally on July

8, 2013, we met our son for the first time. We finalized his adoption on May 21, 2014.

Now when I think back on that time I just look at it as the world's longest pregnancy.

And it was worth every minute, every stretch mark, every piece of paper, every prying question. The waiting. The rejection. The feeling that you just don't measure up. Yes, this process will break your heart every day until one day you walk up the stairs past the room that used to be your bedroom before you turned it into a kid's room and in that moment it will all make sense because there he is, your kid. The kid you adopted. The kid who it feels has always been there.

THROUGH THE LOOKING GLASS

He was waiting for us at the door. I imagine he had been there for days, from the moment his foster parents told him we were coming. With his perfectly parted hair and his blue shirt buttoned to the very top button, he had a smile so big it threatened to swallow the whole of the earth. I suspected his bags were already packed, tucked discreetly behind the door, in anticipation of our arrival. He would have come home with us in that moment had we let him. He would have gone anywhere with us in that moment. Us, the parents he had been waiting a lifetime to meet.

It had been six weeks since the decision. Some faceless committee on the other side of the country deciding our future and creating our family. From the start all we had been given was a basic narrative and a photo. It's the photo that gets you. It's the photo that dares you to imagine a lifetime of birthdays and Christmases and bedtime hugs. It's the photo that teases you with a tomorrow that may never happen.

That photo. It invades your dreams. It speaks to you. It sometimes calls you Dad.

I had that photo, his photo, on my computer, but I tried not to look at it, afraid that I would go even further down the rabbit hole. Without the photo he was just a collection of words; a story with a beginning, middle and a distant end. Without the photo, I could close the book, put it back on the shelf. Without the photo he was not real.

Except he *was* real and I had already imagined all of the birthdays and the Christmases and the lifetime of hugs. I heard his voice call me Dad. I pictured a future with him, my son -- this boy I'd never met. And that was dangerous. Because the faceless committee on the other side of the country deciding our future might have hated us. They could have chosen another family, a better match.

Of course, that wasn't the case. They chose us.

We traveled backward through four time zones, arriving in Oregon shortly after we had left Pittsburgh. It was a few miles from the hotel to his foster home and as we drove I remember looking over at my husband and thinking, *This is the last time it will be just the two of us.* In a few minutes, for the rest of our lives, it would now be the three of us (at least).

I closed the car door and rounded the corner to the house. Everything changed.

In the movies and in books when writers employ that laziest of clichés *love at first sight* (see chapter three), I always roll my eyes and silently chastise the author for condescending to his audience with weak plot devices. "Show, don't tell!" I want to scream as I throw the book across the room. "This isn't real life!" I say as I shake my fists in protest at the movie screen.

People do not fall in love at first sight. Except for parents. Parents fall in love at first sight. From the moment they see their child they are in love. And it does not matter if they are seeing a newborn or a seven year old, that love is immediate and unconditional and eternal.

The moment I saw my son standing at that door -- with his perfectly parted hair and his blue shirt buttoned to the very top button and his smile so big it threatened to swallow the whole of the earth -- I was in love. We may have lived in two different worlds for the first seven years of his life, but he was my son as sure as if I had made him. Looking at him I realized that every moment in my life before this moment had been nothing more than an audition.

Curtain up.

He opened the door, offering his hand to me in greeting. It had been a rehearsed bit meant to show respect, but also a subtle wink from his foster parents to let me know that they had done their job, that he had manners. He shook with his left hand. I shook with my right hand. It was very awkward, less of a hand shake and more of a hand embrace. Just another reason to love him.

He had decided that I would be called *Dad* and Todd would be *Papa*. "I'm Christopher," he said.

My son, Christopher. And me, his Dad. Was I really someone's Dad?

We made our way to the living room and sat on the couch, my husband on the left and me on the right with our son between us as if he had always been there. A camera appeared, immortalizing our first moments as a family. The picture captures two smiling grown men, wide-eyed and deliriously happy, and a young boy, home at last. The photo sits in my son's room. Sometimes I find myself staring at that photo and suddenly I am inside the picture, living a memory as if today were yesterday and yesterday were now.

I hear my son reading to us. I can't remember the name of the book, just the sound of his voice. The voice I first imagined before there was a voice, when all I had was a photo and a collection of words. Christopher, Chris, sits across from me, his face buried in his book as he reads with tentative confidence. I close my eyes and his voice takes me out of the room, out of the house, past the hotel, past tomorrow, fast forwarding me through a life that has yet to happen. We are on the plane, back in Pittsburgh, at our home. He is eight, nine, eighteen, twenty-seven years old. There are birthdays and Christmases and a lifetime of hugs. No longer a child, now a man. From the beginning of our story to the end of mine. He reads and I see it all.

In July of 2013, my husband and I traveled to Oregon to meet our son for the first time. It was the beginning of a life-changing adventure. Five days later when we boarded a plane back to Pittsburgh with our soon-to-be-adopted then-seven year old son in tow, we were a family. Sometimes everything just falls into place. Sometimes *love at first sight* transcends cliché. Sometimes only a stale platitude will do: *it was meant to be.*

MY TWO DADS

Chris had been living with us for less than a month that Sunday morning he first stumbled into our bedroom and exclaimed, "Oh. So that's how you sleep." I'm not sure what he expected to find when he opened the door to our bedroom. I imagine he pictured us in brotherly bunk beds or matching Ozzie and Harriet-style twin beds, me with my hair in pink curlers and Todd smoking a pipe while thumbing through the latest copy of *National Geographic*. Instead he found two middle-aged men at opposite sides of a queen-sized bed, one still half-asleep and the other checking Facebook on his phone. The only thing shocking about the tableau was how pedestrian it was.

If anything, the profoundly dull and unremarkable scene he encountered that morning in our bedroom served to affirm just how much like everyone else we are. We may be two gay guys, but in terms of must-see TV we are a waste of

DVR space. But then our son knew the score; he was well-informed. The situation had been explained to him prior to our meeting. Chris knew he was being adopted by two men and he understood that these two men, his Dad and Papa, were married. It was clear there would be no mother in our family photos. Yet for as much as Chris appeared to understand the realities of his new family, for those first few weeks his brain didn't always make the right connections. We were a puzzle he was still putting together.

There were mornings over breakfast where he would ask me if I planned on marrying a woman and then later that night over dinner he would encourage me to date his yoga teacher. I would remind him that I was already married to his Papa and that while his yoga teacher did have nice hair, she was also a woman and *I was gay* which meant I liked men and besides it was generally considered bad form to date other people while still married. Chris would nod his head, seeming to understand, and then turn to Todd and ask if there was maybe perhaps a special lady in his life. The scenario repeated itself off and on for several months. I briefly considered asking his yoga teacher out for coffee just to shut him up.

It's difficult to explain what it means to be gay to a child who has only ever seen the world through the eyes of heterosexual couples, however open-minded they may have been. It's a world where every love story is between a man and a woman and every well-meaning adult routinely asks a seven year old boy if he has a little girlfriend (because any other option would be unthinkable!)

My son did not cry out for a mother; he never knew one in the traditional sense. But, the heart wants what the eyes see and his eyes had spent a lifetime seeing fathers *and* mothers, first with his grandparents and then with his foster parents. Our family tree was something new.

If this new branch of the tree was going to grow my son would need a g-rated crash course in the LGBTQIA alphabet soup of sexuality. Lesbian Gay Bisexual Transgender Questioning Intersex Asexual. It's confusing and a bit overwhelming, this initialism that just won't end. Before long our gender identity banners will span the length of a city block, reading like a Snellen Eye Chart.

Admittedly, my interest begins and ends at the G. It is how I identify and who I am. The other letters are just that, letters. I imagine I am not alone in this personal failing. If I had to guess, it's a failing I share with many others in the ever-expanding queer community. For many Lesbians I'm sure it begins and ends at the L; for Bisexuals, the B; and for those in the Trans community, it's all about the T.

Not that I was completely ignorant. I had done the odds bits of homework in an attempt to familiarize myself with the LGBTQI and A-s of this sexuality shorthand. In college, I briefly flirted with bisexuality. Once upon a time I read Jeffrey Eugenides' intersex novel *Middlesex*. More recently I cheered on Felicity Huffman as she rode her magical penis to an Oscar nomination in *Transamerica* and I applauded as Jeffrey Tambor embraced his inner vagina on TV's *Transparent*. I even dated a lesbian once in high school.

Surely I could explain this new world to a seven year old. After all as a practicing G, I was a steward of the movement. Inclusivity and understanding must begin with me. The future of the LGBTQIA *Scrabble*-fuck was resting on my shoulders. I could do this.

So I changed the narrative. I told my son stories that included his family dynamic.

"But I don't want you to be gay," he confessed. (He may not be my son biologically, but he was sounding a hell of a lot like my mother.) I assured him I was gay. I told him that once upon a time I had tried to like girls. I held hands with them and kissed them. I even went so far as to imagine a comically tepid future with them complete with disappointing wedding night and accommodating pool boys. I was playing a part in a play that I had not auditioned for and the reviews were in: I was box office poison. But still I tried. And tried. And tried. And tried until one day I stopped trying and then I liked boys. I stopped pretending to be the person I thought I was supposed to be and I started being the person I was. I was gay. It was that simple.

I was pretty pleased with myself. I felt as if I had handled the situation. Score one for the home team. And then my son threw me a curveball or bended it like Beckham or drew an inside straight or whatever the appropriate sports analogy would be in this particular situation.

"Where do babies come from?" he asked. I broke into a cold sweat before stammering that he was too young and promising to discuss the matter further when he was older. I thought back to my own parents. I was eleven or twelve years old the afternoon my Dad gave me *the talk*. We were cleaning out the fish tank and, in my dramatic recollection of events, I was so horrified I put scalding hot water in the tank, boiling several fish alive. After flushing *les poissons morts* down the toilet, my Dad schooled me on the mechanics of sex, heterosexual sex.

It was a pretty standard by-the-book man-woman penis-vagina narrative; much like the one given to every kid since the dawn of time when heterosexuals ruled the Earth. It may not have been the most inclusive narrative, but there was no denying that in terms of baby-making it was true. And thorough.

Where do babies come from? He asked again. I opened a beer and, following a long drink, vaguely explained that men and women have different bodies. He asked me to elaborate and I recall referencing something I termed a "birth hole" shortly before losing consciousness. The third explanation, of which I am not at all proud, sounded as if it had been lifted from the pages of the Marquis de Sade and then staged in the style of the Grand Guignol. The fourth time he asked, I told him the truth.

There was a lengthy pause. "That's awful," he said. Tell me about it, I thought.

A few weeks after the gay baby making incident Chris was watching an animated series about a group of misfit teenage superheroes, most of the PG-13 humor going straight over his head. The scene had featured a boy and a girl sharing a plate of spaghetti, a riff on that classic moment in *Lady & the Tramp*. At the point where the would-be sweethearts are set to kiss, a second boy popped into the scene locking lips with the first boy. "Ew. Gross," my son declared.

"Excuse me," I said in my best *oh-hell-no-you-did-not* inside voice. Time stopped. I considered the moment. It was a cheap joke. *Two boys kissing.* The lazy math of straight comedy writers: (Boy + Boy) x Kissing = Funny.

Ew. Gross.

I asked my son, who by this point had witnessed his fathers share a loving lip-lock on numerous occasions, why it was gross, these two boys kissing. He confessed that the other kids at school had told him that two boys kissing were -- in the schoolyard vernacular of adolescent hate -- gay. Like fat and retarded, gay is the all-purpose go-to insult of children everywhere.

Gay.

You're not okay. You're different.

The fact is my son has two fathers who are gay and there is nothing wrong with being gay. It is no different than being born black or white; it's just what you are. There are people in this world who believe my husband and I should not be parents, that our marriage is invalid, who think the children we have should be taken away from us. For those people the word gay is a weapon; a cheap joke passed from parent to child used to make a little boy feel worthless. Different.

Ew. Gross.

When you say it, you make those people credible. You give them power. You let them win. I said this to him. *You need to stand up for yourself. You need to stand up for your family. Be proud. Always.*

A lot has changed in the two years since we became a family. Chris has successfully put together the puzzle. He may on occasion still crave a maternal presence, but he is fiercely protective and proud of his all boys club. Sometimes at the playground I see him pointing at us and saying to the other kids, "My dads are gay." On a recent family vacation to Puerto Rico he made new friends at the hotel pool by way of announcing, "I have two dads. They're gay." The other kids ate it up, and we became something of a curiosity while he became the coolest kid on the beach.

To an outsider watching it may have appeared that he was using us to show off, and I suppose there is a degree of truth to that, but now when I see him play the gay card I see a once-uncertain boy letting the world know that he is without equivocation proud of his family. My son no longer asks about the business of girlfriends or wives. He no longer exclaims, "Ew. Gross." Now when he speaks, he speaks with confidence, saying: *This is my family. We are just like other families. Do you want to play on the swings?*

THIS AIN'T SHAKESPEARE, KID

We came to parenthood a bit late in the game, adopting Chris when he was seven years old. As a result we missed out on the firsts. We cannot go back in time and live that moment when Chris took his first breath or use our phones to record his first awkward steps or shriek with delight when he uttered his first word or bandage his first skinned knee or hear the first mellifluous measures of his musical laugh. These are moments we will never experience. And it's strange because most days we forget that our son hasn't been with us since that first breath; that he wasn't born from our miracle uterus. I look back into the past and he's always been there.

Our son has rewritten his story too. Chris has a lifetime of experiences that do not include us, but in his faded Xerox memory the stories have been reworked -- details have been shaded, locations shifted, and central roles recast. In his new memories his Papa and I are present. Sometimes we are bystanders, sometimes active participants, sometimes we are his parents. He looks back into the past and we have always been there.

Todd and I share a lifetime of photos. We could fill countless scrapbooks; volumes devoted to our respective births, our terrible twos, the first day of school. But of Chris we have no picture memories before the age of five. We have clues. Fragments of stories shared with us; stories like the time he accidentally spilled spaghetti sauce on the floor and his grandfather beat him with his belt. Or the one about that time when he was three and his sisters lost him in the airport. We have distant narratives written by overworked caseworkers and reports dictated by psychologists who I doubt ever bothered to even look up from their notepads to see the scared little boy in front of them.

I look at our photos and it's easy to remember that we had a life before our son. I read through his files and it's strange to think he had one before us. And if I'm being honest the life he had before us scares me. I worry that one day, when he is much older, that life will steal him away from us. I am intimidated by the shadow of a cherished grandmother who loved him, but could not provide for him. I fear that he will cling to the ghosts of his past out of obligation, or worse, guilt because out of five kids he was the one who was given the new beginning.

One day my son will ask about his birth parents, these two strangers who made him. Like most kids in foster care he did not end up there because life was good. As a general rule of thumb, children are not taken from good parents. Chris had a rough start in life, at one point living in a tent as a baby. He was forgotten and neglected. In the short span of a few years he lived in a half-dozen foster homes, not always with the best people (the exception being his last foster family, an inspiring couple who nurtured his gentleness and made him feel safe and loved). He's seen and experienced things that people ten times his age have never seen or experienced. And while he is the very definition of resilience, one day he will want answers and when that day comes how exactly will I navigate those muddy waters?

I tell myself the past is the past, but then I hear the voice of Shakespeare (or what I imagine to be the voice of Shakespeare—Liza Minnelli) proclaim, "What's past is prologue."

I vow to flip the script. I battle these self-fulfilling prophecies. I find solace in the present and I take comfort in the stories of those who came before us. I believe in signs.

On a recent trip to the grocery store, the destination hotspot for all long-term married couples with an afternoon free from children, Todd and I found ourselves in the checkout line quietly bickering over which cereal to buy. (The things that pass for passion once you've seen each other naked for more than a decade.) The clerk, a high school student who was maybe seventeen years old, interrupted our would-be foreplay and asked, "Are you two partners?" It was an unusual question given the surroundings. I didn't know how to answer or if I should answer. I considered the possibility that he was awkwardly attempting to hit on me while Todd worried that the kid had decided to use us as parental surrogates and was about to practice his coming out speech.

We were both wrong.

The clerk said he was asking because, as it turned out, he had two Dads. He then went on to tell us that his Dads had adopted him…from Oregon (like Chris)…when he was about seven years old (like Chris). He told us how he had spent those first few years of his life in a small town outside of Portland (like Chris) living with his grandparents (like Chris) before being placed in foster care (again, like Chris) and then at last being adopted by two gay guys from Pittsburgh (like, well, you get the point). The similarities were stunning.

But what struck more than the similarities, more than these coincidences, were the odds that we had found ourselves at this particular grocery store on this particular day in this particular line being waited on by this particular clerk who then, for whatever reason, felt a connection to us which prompted him to share his story, which in many ways was our son's story.

It was as if we had stepped through a door into the future. The clerk – a tall, lanky, dark-haired boy – was the very picture of what I imagined Chris will be at seventeen. As the clerk talked, it wasn't the clerk telling his story, it was *Chris* telling *our* story. It was as if the universe was opening a door and telling us, "Past is not always prologue."

In that moment I wanted to meet this young man's parents. These two men who adopted this seven year old boy from Oregon. I wanted to shake their hands and to thank them for coming before me. For blazing the trail. For giving this young man a home and a future that included reassuring hugs, and goodnight kisses, and evenings playing board games, and extravagant Christmas mornings, and love, and happiness, and a million other things I hope to give my children.

As the clerk handed me my receipt and thanked us for shopping at the store I found myself asking him if he was happy. It was an odd question, invasive really, and I silently judge myself for being so forward. But he seemed to think nothing of it and replied, "Yes. I'm very happy." And for some reason that made me very happy.

I thought back to the birth of my niece. Todd and I were present (this was before we had our own children). She was beautiful, this new life, a miniature version of who my sister once was, but also the person she could still be. Endless possibilities. And my sister would get to be a part of it all from the first moment -- the first breath, the first word, the first everything. I was deeply jealous.

When I look at photos of my niece there is no mistaking that she is her mother's daughter. It's in her face, her eyes, her nose, her hair, her smile. My son will never have my DNA. He will never have my husband's cute nose or his flat feet. My son has the genes of strangers. But what he lacks in our nature he has adopted in our nurture. The dry sense of humor, the dramatic sense of self, the way he dismisses a situation with a single glance.

One day my son will confront his past and the truth will change him, but it will not define him because we are all more than where we began. So our son doesn't have our DNA. So we get stuck with the less desirable firsts like first heartbreak and first horrible teenage meltdown. It doesn't matter. Because in the end he may not be of us, but he is us.

EYE OF THE TIGER

Chris had left his backpack in the car. Again. He does this a lot, leaving things behind. His backpack, his lunchbox, his gloves. Last summer he came home from day camp in just his bathing suit, having lost his clothes, shoes and spare eyeglasses while at the pool. It's to the point that whenever I walk down the stretch of alley between my office and the coffee shop and I see a single shoe or a stray pair of pants I think, "Chris must have been here."

I looked at the forgotten backpack in the backseat of the car and sighed. The phone rang. It was Chris. I assumed he was calling to ask me to bring the backpack to school. Having previously vowed to never again chauffeur his backpack ten miles across town to his school, I let it go to voicemail.

My son has a lot of feelings. There is no pretense with Chris. He is emotionally honest. If he is sad, he cries. If he is happy, he laughs. If he is angry, he stomps his feet and then makes this weird huffing sound. He keeps it simple.

I listened to the message. He was hysterical. There were tears and unintelligible sobs and carefully-constructed whispered declarations of revenge against someone named Corey. I imagined the scene in the school office: My son, the Susan Lucci of Liberty Elementary, bursts into the school office tearfully demanding to use the phone. The school secretary, a tragically permed woman who is not paid enough money to put up with this kind of crap, tries to calm him down. Chris is having none of her hollow consolations. This is his moment. Clutching the broken glasses, he plays his scene to the last row in the balcony, delivering a monologue worth ten Daytime Emmys.

I had to play the message several times in order to piece together all the details before I had the whole story. A classmate had accidentally broken Chris's glasses. Chris loves his glasses. He had selected his first set of blinkers, a pair of on-point black rimmed hipster style frames, when he was just six years old. A year later when we took him to get new glasses he chose a pair of blue and black tortoise shell frames that were, in a word, fabulous. It was the tortoise shell glasses he had lost at the pool. It was the much-loved black hipster frames the classmate had broken.

As much as Chris took pride in his glasses, I suspect his (over)reaction had less to do with breaking them and more to do with what those particular glasses had represented. They were a tangible link to his life in Oregon. When those glasses broke a part of his past slipped away.

The day went from bad to worse when we picked up Chris from the bus stop and discovered that not only had his glasses been broken, he had also lost them at some point during the day. This realization was followed by an epic three-hour homework showdown where Chris declared that 12 divided by 4 was 27 and a comma went at the end of a sentence,

Some days.

Later as I tucked him into bed it was clear the day's events had finally caught up to him. He admitted that he felt stupid for losing his glasses, for not understanding his homework, for having a bad day. *We all have bad days, but you get through them.* Chris has already been through so much that wasn't good; the earliest years of his life highlighted by chaos and a revolving door of homes and foster placements. *Everything that came before, that was the hard stuff.* Not forgetting your gloves, making sure you have your backpack, remembering to read the directions on your homework -- that was the easy stuff. *You can do the easy stuff.*

Life is hard even when you're eight years old. And some days really do feel like the worst days of your life. I am proud of Chris's emotional honesty. Still, I worry that this emotional freedom will get him into trouble. I worry he will give his heart away too easily only to have it returned broken in a million pieces. I worry that others will see him as an easy mark and take advantage of his kind heart. I worry that he is too good, too compassionate.

It was his eighth birthday. We were planning his party and we told him he could invite ten people from his class. After selecting the A-group of best friends, he passed over those in the B-group of good friends in favor of inviting a boy who had spent the better part of the school year tormenting him. I asked Chris why he wanted to invite this boy who had been so mean to him and Chris said, "I don't think he has a lot of friends." I hear him say this and I wonder is my son Gandhi or the guy that bought the Brooklyn Bridge?

And whether he is the former or the latter, I worry people will mistake that same heart he wears on his sleeve for weakness and underestimate his strength and his ability to survive. Or worse, I worry he may change and become just like the rest of us. Someone asks us how we are doing and, even on the worst day of our life, we reply, *I'm fine.* We routinely assure our friends that we are *happy*, leaving off the qualifier: *enough.* We smile through our anger and laugh through our tears. We swallow our rage and scream into pillows. Is it simply that, unlike the rest of us, Chris has not yet learned to pretend? I hope he never learns to pretend. I hope if he needs to scream, he screams -- not into a pillow -- but out loud for all the world to hear. I hope Chris has the courage and wisdom to always be the person he is right now: a boy who believes in the power of wishing wells and shooting stars.

Because wishes do come true.

Chris had grown up with three half-sisters. He later lived in a home with seven foster siblings. Brothers and sisters were the rule; his life with us as an only child had been the exception. Chris had never been shy about his feelings on the subject and from the beginning he had made it very clear to us that he wanted a sibling. We told him a second adoption would take time. It could be months or even years before he had a brother or sister.

Chris decided to take matters into his own hands. He was not about to wait months or years. He tightly closed his eyes, blowing out the candles on his birthday cake. He wanted a brother. He asked Santa, making it number one on his Christmas list. He wanted a brother. He wished at every well, hoping on every star and eyelash. He wanted a brother.

When we told Chris that the adoption agency had matched us with a child -- someone who, if everything fell into place, might very possibly be his brother in a few weeks or months -- he stopped eating his dinner, smiled a smile the width of his face, and then, shrieking with delight, announced that he had never been happier. The universe had granted his wish.

And then without warning the smile faded as the shrieking dissolved into tears. Chris is a very messy crier, but these were sloppier, more hysterical tears; these were Oscar-winning tears. Todd and I looked at each other in confusion. *Wasn't this what he wanted?* Chris assured us he was fine, telling us "I just need to be alone for a few minutes."

And so he went up to his room to be alone. *Because he has a lot of feelings.*

~~Like any good stage mother not wanting to miss out on a moment of the drama, I counted to almost sixty before rushing up the stairs, two at a time, to get the full story.~~ I mean, like a good parent, I respected his need for privacy and allowed him several minutes to compose himself before checking on him. I found him perched on the ladder of his loft bed, sobbing uncontrollably.

"What's wrong?" I asked.

"I'm just so happy," he sobbed through his hysterical tears.

"But you're crying," I said.

"I know," he agreed.

"Are you okay?" I asked.

"This is the happiest day of my life," he said.

And because he's honest, I knew he meant it.

THE STORY OF US

Chris's adoption became finalized 318 days after he was first placed with us. Todd and I had always wanted more than one child so the decision to adopt again upon Chris's finalization was an easy one. Still, we needed to wait until Chris was ready. He may have expressed an eagerness to have a sibling early on, but *wanting* a brother and *having* a brother were two different things. It was important he felt secure in his (still) new home; the last thing we wanted was for Chris to feel like he was being replaced with a newer model.

Chris had spent half his life in the foster system. He had witnessed countless foster siblings come and go over the years, some kids returning to their former homes with old families and others being placed in new homes with new families. He may have been just a child but Chris was experienced well beyond his immature years in the fundamental inner workings of the foster system. Still, navigating the system from the perspective of a waiting parent would be very different from that of a waiting child. Chris wanted a brother yesterday. In adoption, nothing happens yesterday. This would take time. By putting ourselves back into the process we would be subject to more paperwork, more background checks, more home visits, more unanswered emails, and of course more waiting.

Over the next several months our caseworker sent us approximately a dozen profiles, but none of the children proved a suitable match to our new family dynamic. There were children with a history of aggression toward other children, children with extreme emotional issues, children who were in the habit of setting fires. It had been challenging enough to match a child to us when it was just Todd and me, but now we had to consider Chris.

We independently inquired after more than fifty kids of various ages and races from all over the country. The profiles we were working from, the profiles provided to all waiting families, are intentionally vague. They are outlines of a rough sketch full of curious omissions that force you to read between the lines. The majority of our independent inquiries proved to be dead ends with no return response from the children's caseworkers. I chose to believe that *most* of our inquiries went unanswered because we simply were not the right match for the child, and not because we were a same-sex couple.

Of course most is not all. There were exceptions. Over time we learned to avoid certain states. A pattern quickly emerged: if a state was poor, conservative and in the south the likelihood was that we would be politely informed that it was essential for the child to have both a mother and a father. We were never told why this was essential, just that it was essential. A caseworker from Utah informed us that he would have been happy to match us with two boys, but he knew with absolute certainty that no judge in Utah would ever sign off on a gay adoption. I wasn't offended; I appreciated his honesty.

We had naïvely assumed that due to the success of our first adoption caseworkers would be lining up to work with us. As summer days at the pool gave way to fall and a return to school I reminded myself that *the waiting is only bad when you are actually waiting.* We took Chris to visit Santa Claus a few days after Thanksgiving. "I want a brother," he said.

A few weeks later our caseworker presented us with a profile for the hobbit (so nicknamed because of his extremely short stature; at five years old he barely measured three feet tall). After the mountains of additional paperwork, after the second round of tedious home visits, after the endless months of waiting we had been matched with a child. The plan was for Todd and me to meet with the hobbit's caseworkers in two weeks. Until then, it would be more waiting.

In adoption, nothing is ever a done deal until the last stack of papers are signed and notarized. As excited as I was about this new development I knew I had to keep quiet because there were no guarantees. The fact is we were one of two families being considered for this adoption, so while there was a 50/50 chance that we would have the privilege of being the hobbit's parents, I needed to think more along the lines of 99/1 with 99 being the likelihood that it would not happen and 1 being the chance that everything in the universe would align and despite a billion to one odds two gay guys would get to be parents a second time.

I'm terrible with secrets. If someone says to me, "I have to tell you something but you have to promise not tell anyone else," I will immediately develop diarrhea of the mouth. The phrase *just between the two of us* sends me into a texting frenzy. Confidence is something you have, not something you share. I don't mean to be a gossip. I just don't like to be burdened and frankly if you need to confess find a priest.

I lasted a full 48 1/2 hours with our secret before I spilled the beans. I knew that announcing it and making it real was like telling everyone you're pregnant the day after your period is late. Metaphorically we had done all the work -- taken temperatures, charted ovulation cycles, intercoursed -- but we still had to meet with the stork. The best I could do for now was throw my legs up in the air and let nature take its course. The plan was to meet with the caseworkers in two weeks and then a few days after that we'd know for sure if we had been much blessed.

In the days leading up to the big meeting we worked on our *Life Book*. A Life Book is just fancy adoption-speak for scrapbook. The word scrapbook causes me great anxiety. It makes my ass itch and my foot twitch. I know there are many people who scrapbook as a way to relax and to those people I say, "Have you ever tried cutting?" Personally if I want to relax I'll wash down a few pills with a glass of wine (not really), but hey, to each his own.

The Life Book is meant to tell the story of your family. The story of us. The first step in life booking is to select your photos. Fortunately we have become the sort of people who take pictures of everything: *Chris eating a sandwich! Sean watching TV! Todd reading a book!* We chose more than two hundred photos in round one, but less than fifty made the final cut. The next step was to buy supplies. Now if you are the kind of person who becomes anxious at the mere mention of the word scrapbook, then you should probably never under any circumstance go shopping for scrapbook supplies.

Scrapbooking is a multi-billion dollar industry. Seriously. People who scrapbook are not fucking around. Entire sections of craft stores are devoted to the art of the scrapbook. There are themed background papers, three-dimensional stickers, color-coordinated letter sets, photo corners, and sticky glue tabs. The album itself will set you back a week's pay.

After emptying out our 401Ks and taking a second mortgage on the house, we commenced life booking. It really is quite difficult to sum up your entire life in ten pages; even more so when you know someone is going to decide whether or not you get to be parents based partly on those ten pages. In theory we were making this book for a five year old as a means of introduction, but in reality the book was being designed for the committee as a means by which to judge us.

We obsessed over photos and layout and color themes and which three-dimensional stickers we should use as if that alone would be the deciding factor. *We were going to let you have the child but then we noticed that you mixed fonts on page seven which suggests to us a certain level of chaos that might not be healthy for such a young child.*

Seventy-two hours later and -- after all the anxiety, all the shouting, all the door slamming, all the tears -- we had done it. We had effectively marketed ourselves. Page after page of happy smiling faces, laughter, love...and stickers. Lots of stickers.

As I walked through the pages of our story, I considered the challenges of our situation. We were two men trying to make omelets without eggs. As I mourned the absence of our magical baby-making vagina, I realized we had something so much better: we had a really expensive scrapbook with stickers.

The meeting took place on a Tuesday. I spent the night before practicing my smile in the mirror and changing costumes, I mean outfits. We didn't know what to expect. I assumed they would ask us a bunch of questions and then I imagined we would engage in some sort of *Hunger Games*-esque battle with the other couple. I'd be a sexier Jennifer Lawrence and Todd would be whichever character wore the most ridiculous wig. Or maybe it was more like *Mad Max* and whoever emerged from the Thunderdome wearing a Tina Turner mask got the kid.

I hated to think of it as a competition, but isn't that exactly what it was? Because someone was going to win and someone else was going to lose. After all the questions and paperwork and Life Book submissions, one family would simply be a better match. One family would possess the skills and resources that best met the hobbit's needs. And even then it wouldn't be about who was best, but who was better in this situation. *It was an honor just to be nominated*, I told myself, not meaning it.

The committee was made up of five women. They were incredibly friendly, making us feel welcome from the moment we walked in the door. I sensed that we were something of a novelty and Todd theorized that maybe we were a test case as West Virginia had just legalized gay marriage. The committee seemed positively giddy to be interviewing two men and I imagined them trying to out-progressive their liberal friends, bragging about us at their next dinner party.

Dinner Guest: I did the Virginia Reel with Rachel Maddow at a lesbian barn dance.

Committee Member 1: Really? Well, we just gave two gay guys a kid.

Committee Member 2: Check and mate, bitches.

I don't remember what they asked us. There may have been no questions. I think we just talked. We told them about our lives and how we met and all about Chris. There was a lot of smiling and nodding. It occurred to us that this meeting was a formality. Eventually it was their turn to talk. They told us about the hobbit, this boy we had never met who two hours later would be our son.

Our son, Elijah.

There was no second family. They had already chosen us.

It's hard to describe the moment when they tell you. You hear the words but they don't seem real. This thing you have been waiting for your whole life -- this thing that has already happened once can't be happening again because no one ever wins the lottery twice in one lifetime. Except for us.

NO MORE GOODBYES

We got the kid. *We got the kid.* I had to keep saying it to make it real. I was in shock. It happened so fast I kept expecting someone to jump out from the backseat of the van and scream, "Just kidding!" You wait and wait and wait and then wait some more, but when it finally does happen, it happens fast. One minute you're driving across state lines toward an uncertain future and then three hours later you're in IKEA trying to decide which bed to buy for the five year old you've never met who's moving into your house in a few weeks. The reality slowly begins to take hold twenty-four hours later when you find yourself making a scene in Target because they're all out of monogrammed letter "E" Christmas stockings.

The weekend before Christmas is typically a last-minute frenzy of holiday shopping and cookie baking. This year it was the weekend I met my son. The meeting took place in a house that had once been home to some member of the privileged class, some elite West Virginian who would turn over in his grave if he could see that his once-beloved house had been turned into a government office. We arrived early to the meeting, allowing us time to freak out (me), ask a million questions (Chris), and stand stoically (Todd). The tension was building and before we could default to our argument setting, he arrived.

We watched from the glass-enclosed former sunroom as Elijah made his grand entrance from the side door of a gray minivan. As he jumped from the vehicle I laughed. He was comically undersized. His foster mother brought him into the office and Chris immediately pounced on him with a battery of questions before forcing Elijah to sit down so he could show (read: narrate) the Life Book.

We retired to the playroom (the former parlor, if I had to guess) with two of Elijah's caseworkers who would assist in the transition over the next few weeks. Elijah would not live with us until the interstate adoption papers were in order. For now he would continue to live with his foster mother and we would have weekend visitations.

At first, Elijah would not look at us. He just sat on the floor playing with his toy cars. He said a few words, part of a brief narrative directed at and for the benefit of his toys. Barely five years old and already he had mastered the art of freezing people out. The minutes ticked by slowly, passing into hours. We didn't exist. I freaked out. Chris asked more questions. Todd, no longer standing, now sat stoically.

And then something clicked and the four of us came together. Suddenly Chris and Elijah were running around the office engaged in an endless game of hide-n-seek. Suddenly I was hiding under the desk with Elijah, having been roped into the game. Suddenly Elijah was holding Todd's hand as we walked to the car. Then we were at the zoo and Elijah was following Chris everywhere, shouting "Chris! Chris!" as he chased after the big brother who seemed to have been there his whole life.

For me it was in that moment when Elijah asked me to carry him, because now I could be trusted. It was after Elijah fell and Todd scooped him up into his arms and cradled him, both looking as if they were finally home. It was the sight of two sleeping brothers curled up together in a hotel bed.

And so it went for the next few weeks. The uncertainty. The transition. A weekend here and a few days there. Everything was temporary. Life was suspended. Time was reduced to a series of visits. We stole moments. We created false realities. We were our best selves, which is to say, not our true selves.

While the states of Pennsylvania and West Virginia were busy crossing their respective t's, we were trying to become a family; not the easiest thing to do when you are basically living under the terms of a 30-day money back guarantee. We may have been selected as his forever family, but there was still the chance his placement with us would not be permanent. For six weeks we shuffled back and forth between Pittsburgh and Wheeling (and on a few occasions, points further south of *Deliverance*). Weekend meetings at hotels off the interstate gave way to weekend meetings at our house off the interstate. It was all very clandestine. Saturday and Sunday came and went and then Monday it was back to reality.

It was hard. We were working to establish a relationship, learning trust and affection through shared experiences and memories. We were learning not just to know one another, but how to know one another. Yet no matter how often we would see each other, no matter how much progress we had made on a previous visit, each time was the first time. We were characters in a play rehearsing until we got it right. Every Friday was the read through, Saturday the dress rehearsal, and then just as the curtain was coming up on the Sunday matinee it was time to say goodbye.

The goodbyes were the worst. You can't explain goodbyes to a five year old. Or an eight year old. Not when you the adult don't understand them yourself. So we would say goodbye and Elijah didn't mind. At first. But then he wanted to stay, except he couldn't because that would have been kidnapping. He may have been ours, but not really. Not yet. So, goodbye. And Chris would cry. Because he has a lot of feelings. Goodbye. And Todd would get very quiet. Goodbye. *I don't want to go.* Goodbye, until that moment 43 days after we first met him when there would be no more goodbyes.

It was the Christmas we received a very unusual gift: an almost-but-not-quite five-year-old boy named Elijah. We survived the waiting, the interview, the first meeting, the visits back and forth. We survived the goodbyes. There were moments of doubt. *Is this going to work? What if this doesn't work? Does he like us? What if he doesn't like us? Can we do this a second time? No really, can we do this a second time?*

There were raised voices and tears and disagreements.

It's never easy, even when it is.

But there was also laughter. And reluctant hugs turned willing. Suddenly hands weren't asked for, they were given. *I love you* was whispered like a secret gift.

The four of us together made sense. It was easy. In the future there would be bumps in the road, big and little. There would be days when Elijah and Chris would hate each other and nights where Elijah would cry for his foster mother. There would be moments where my son wished he were anywhere but here with us. But we would get past those moments, just as we had with Chris. And just as we had with Chris, we would hold on to the moments when it all felt right.

CRYING ON THE TOILET
AND OTHER BATHROOM DISTRACTIONS

The difference between five and nine is greater than
four. We learned this new math in the days and weeks
following Elijah's placement with us. I had imagined a five
year old would arrive factory ready -- just plug him in, flip
the switch and *presto!* you have a fully functioning mini
humanoid. This is untrue. It turns out five year olds are
basically talking babies that can use the toilet. You still have
to bathe them, dress them, tie their shoes, hold their hands in
public, teach them to read, force them to nap, force them to
brush their teeth, monitor them as they brush their teeth, and
clean up after they brush their teeth, and while they may be
able to talk the toilet business is 50/50 on a good day.

Chris was a breeze in comparison. Granted he was a few
years older, so he could be trusted to take a bath, dress
himself and not run out into traffic. Elijah was another story.
He was exhausting. He required constant attention. I laugh at

the former me who once considered adopting a child under the age of three. *I could absolutely handle a newborn*, I bragged to my friends and family. If an all-things-considered-well-behaved five year old nearly drove me to the brink a newborn would have killed me.

And Elijah is a good kid. Oh sure sometimes he pees his pants while waiting in line at the amusement park but otherwise he's fairly continent. He is an average five year old who listens 75% of the time and hates napping. He has never once been horrible in public, which is more than I could say for those non-GMO-gluten-free-Paleo kids I see at the mall. (And for the record, I see you other parents judging me when my son eats his genetically modified deep-fried sugar-dipped potato-in-a-bun.) Elijah may ask a million questions but he asks them because he's curious. He wants to learn. There is no end to his inquisition: *What are clouds? Where does the moon sleep? Do girls have wieners?* I do my best to answer his questions, but I also recognize that I am not an expert in meteorology, astronomy or female anatomy.

The endless questions were nothing compared to the boundless energy and I began to fear that I had met my match. Here I was a forty year old man and my undoing would be at the hands of a five year old. Elijah had been with us for about two weeks the Sunday afternoon I fell victim to a plate of questionable Middle Eastern kebabs. Food poisoning is never pleasant and I spent the better part of the night projectile vomiting the previous day's spaghetti dinner.

The next morning I awoke dehydrated with a blinding headache. If it had been just me I could have managed the situation. I would have popped a few aspirin, confined myself to the couch and slept the day away. But it wasn't just me. It was me and a five year old (due to a clerical error Elijah was still not enrolled in school). Todd had gone back to work the previous week and now I was on daddy duty, food poisoning be damned.

Five year olds don't understand being sick. They don't understand blinding headaches and dehydration. They cannot be left to their own devices while you cough your best Camille in some faraway Bavarian sanatorium. Five year olds want to play and be five. Five year olds do not want to sit quietly and watch *Law & Order* reruns all day. They instead prefer to run through the house singing at top volume and pretending to be a Disney princess. At least that's what my five year old preferred to do on this particular day. When I suggested we take a nap after his 437th encore of *Let It Go*, he laughed at me. My five year old son laughed at me and then he threw all forty pounds of his little body onto my stomach which at this point, now void of food, had begun to digest my internal organs.

It was sometime around 2:45 p.m. that I excused myself to the bathroom where I cried for seven and a half peaceful minutes.

I do this a lot now. I excuse myself to the bathroom and I cry. The bathroom is my sanctuary. I have spent the better part of an hour holed up behind its locked door, watching videos on my phone or reading the back of the shampoo bottle. Sometimes I turn on the water and I pretend I'm taking a shower. Sometimes I slip down into the bubbles and let *Calgon* take me away. Sometimes I fall asleep on the toilet.

I would kill for a midday nap. I think most adults wish they could indulge in a nap at some point during the day. But children hate naps. If I tell Elijah to take a nap he will collapse on the floor and begin to sob uncontrollably. The first time he did this I hurriedly closed all the windows in the house, afraid that the neighbors would think I was beating him. Now if I even mention the word nap he launches into a five-act opera entitled *Emotionally Unstable Italian Grandmother at the Funeral of Her Dead Husband.*

The truth is we're still figuring him out. He's an odd little kid; he thinks it's hilarious to look you directly in the eyes when you're speaking to him and then do the exact opposite of what you just told him to do even though you're sure he heard you because, after all, he was looking you directly in the eyes when you were talking to him. He also loves to repeat everything you say except for those moments when he's pretending not to hear you. He eats nothing but chicken nuggets with mustard. Give him a choice between eating a plate of fresh vegetables and being water boarded by Dick Cheney and he'd go with virtual drowning by Darth Vader.

If Chris is the very definition of resilience, then Elijah is the very definition of obstinance.

But still, he makes me laugh. His preschool teacher remarked that she had never before met a five year old who understood sarcasm…and then used it. His caseworker noted in his file that Elijah was "a chameleon". She said, "He could adapt to any environment and would often assume the personalities of those around him." It was no doubt a coping mechanism he had adopted, the result of having lived in so many different homes.

In the foster home where he lived before, Elijah had been taught that physical affection was unacceptable; there were no hugs or goodnight kisses. He adapted to this environment and learned to live without affection. When we met him Elijah was emotionally reserved, if not aloof and frosty. He forbade us to hug or kiss him for those first few months. One night before bed he told me that I could not kiss him on the cheek because "boys don't kiss". *They do in this house*, I said, but respected his wishes. Finally after months of watching us shower Chris with affection Elijah changed his outlook. Now he hugs first and when we tuck the boys into bed he demands to be kissed goodnight.

Time moves slowly when you are living inside a moment. In the time before hugs and kisses Elijah would only call us by our first names; it seemed we would never be Dad and Papa. We never forced the issue. If he was comfortable calling us Sean and Todd then he could call us Sean and Todd. Still, when addressing one another in front of him we always referred to each other as Dad and Papa. We instructed Chris to do the same when talking about us to Elijah. We laid the groundwork and it took time, but eventually Elijah began to experiment with our new names until those new names became our only names. Now every morning he wakes me up by crawling into bed and whispering mischievously into my ear, "Daddy!" Now he rushes Todd at the door and with open arms delivers a welcoming, "Papa!" No longer Sean and Todd, now it seems we are who we have always been, his Dad and Papa.

He has become so much like the three of us; it's hard to know who he is *after* us especially when we never knew who he was *before* us. Our obstinate little chameleon has now assumed our manner of speaking, our casual attitude, our sense of humor. Unfortunately he has also adopted some of Chris's less desirable qualities, like selective laziness. Long gone are the days when Elijah would voluntarily (and thoroughly) clean up after himself. We've said goodbye to the boy who eagerly offered to set the dinner table. Now we're left with the pint-sized smartass who, when asked to carry more than one bag of groceries into the house, indignantly replies, "I only have two hands".

The difference between five and nine is still greater than four. But with each whisper of *Daddy*, with each offer of *I love you*, with each willing hug that difference shrinks. Chris and Elijah wanted a forever home, but what they received in the bargain was so much more than a roof and four walls. They found each other. Elijah idolizes Chris and has assumed the role of loyal companion and much smaller shadow. And Chris, the boy who wanted an older brother, has himself taken that role and become the defender, confidante and best friend.

GLADYS KRAVITZ
DOESN'T LIVE HERE ANYMORE

We should have known better. Chris is a world-class gossip. The original Gladys Kravitz. He loves to let the cat out of the bag, beginning each story with "My Dad told me not to tell you this because it's a secret, but..." He routinely gives the game away, revealing what your birthday gift is going to be six months before he has me buy it for you. If you ask him how his day was he will tell you all the things that everyone else did as if the goings-on at his elementary school were worthy of a subplot on *Scandal*.

Children hear everything, or rather, children hear everything you don't want them to hear. Look a child directly in the eyes and give him a specific set of instructions and he will act like you're an alien having just dropped from another planet speaking a strange language of clicks and beeps, but have a private conversation with your significant other behind closed doors two states away and he not only hears every word, he commits it to memory.

It was unfair of us to be angry with Chris. After all, we were guilty. We had said all the things he later repeated to his teacher. Arguably some of our points had been valid, while others were nothing more than the biting observations of two bitchy sarcastic homosexual know-it-alls. Still, I would be lying if I said I wasn't pleased when Chris restated our position; if nothing else it meant he was listening.

We had just sat down to dinner, each of us telling the others about his day. Chris told us about a new reading program his school had instituted. The program mandated that children read one hour every day, including weekends; it was some *No Child Left Behind* ridiculousness left over from George W. Bush's reign of terror. The kids were to read (from a specific government-approved book list) under the supervision of a parent with no distractions, meaning all televisions, phones and computers in the house were to be switched off during the 60-minute reading period. The idea was noble, but for a parent with other children in the home who is already juggling extra-curricular activities with an additional 60 to 90 minutes of homework a night, the program was laughable.

We said it was impossible. Actually we said much worse. We mocked the program and then we mocked the teacher, and while we may have landed a few choice zingers, our belly laughs came at the expense of our dignity when the next day at school Chris repeated to his teacher word for word the contents of our blustery bombast.

The whole situation was a tad humiliating, but the fallout made me realize that children are incredibly impressionable. Apparently I could say anything and my kids would take it as gospel. And this appealed to my vanity. We may want our children to form their own opinions fostered by their unique experiences but, if we're being honest, we also want them to be just like us. In our imagined future reality our children enthusiastically parrot our views and passionately espouse our beliefs. They embrace our opinions on faith and politics. They share our taste in movies and TV. They are the miniature carbon copy of our best self.

Except our children are not miniature carbon copies. Differences abound.

The high school football hero is gifted with the son who loves song and dance. The mother who played Lady Macbeth at Juilliard watches the daughter who plays third base at the local ball field. The bohemian artists give birth to a math nerd. Campaign workers for Eugene McCarthy fall in love and thirty-five years later their offspring work to re-elect George W. Bush.

We all have our crosses to bear.

My moment on the cross proved to be a trip to the amusement park. I hate amusement parks. I hate the lines. I hate the $24 pizza. I hate the way every ride makes me sick. But still I go because my kids love amusement parks. They love the pizza, the rides, even the lines. So I smile, sign over my paycheck, and then discreetly vomit into every available trash can throughout the park.

This is what I agreed to the day I became a Dad. Hidden in a clause of an addendum of a codicil of the adoption paperwork in tiny print I agreed to forfeit my right to have likes and dislikes. We've all done it. After a while we stop reading the fine points and just initial as indicated by the green arrow. (For those of you who came to parenthood the old-fashioned way I suspect this forfeiture agreement was contained in your mortgage documents.) I am convinced that in addition to signing the adoption papers, I also agreed to several high interest loans and swore an eternal blood oath wherein I agreed to be a present and active participant in any and all of my child's activities, regardless of my level of interest, and that I would in addition find my child to be the most interesting aspect of said activity.

A few days after enduring the indignities of the amusement park we took Elijah to the playground. We were meant to be playing on the swings but instead he wandered over to the hockey rink. He watched for the better part of an hour as two junior teams passed the puck back and forth. Later as we walked to the car, he expressed an interest in playing deck hockey. "Great!" I thought, "Now I have to pretend to watch sports for the next thirteen years."

I hate sports.

A week later I was in the basement of a quaint country church watching the back of Chris's head perform in what I would generously call the single worst theatrical production ever staged in the basement of a quaint country church. The real stars of the show were the parents who sat there with polite smiles plastered across their faces pretending to be entertained. Later in the car I told my son the best part of the show was the back of his head.

Some days I dream of a substitute parent. A proxy. A stand-in. A surrogate. A designated hitter. The understudy. In the event a parent is unable (or unwilling) to fulfill his/her parental obligations, the role of the parent will be played by the understudy. I'm not suggesting a total abdication of parental responsibility. The understudy would only go on in the most extreme circumstances, like golf or a grade school production of *Fiddler on the Roof.*

I imagine a conversation with Elijah: "Well son, I wish I could attend your athletic sporting event but as you know the season premiere of *[insert the name of a PBS miniseries]* is on tonight so unfortunately I have to send my regrets. However -- good news! -- my understudy will go on in my place. Now you don't need to worry because he knows everything about athletic sporting events and he loves balls almost as much as I do."

Never again would parents feel the need to pretend. No more obligation. No more forced smiling through the tortures of bad community theater. No more nodding as if you understood the difference between a field goal and a two-point conversion. No more Christmases acting as if you still love your children even though they are now Republicans.

Of course if you give up on those moments, you give up on everything. You miss the moments that make the child. Like that flash after she scores the winning goal and suddenly understands the value of teamwork and sportsmanship. Or the night he learns confidence by overcoming his stage fright when he brings an audience to laughter with a perfectly timed joke. Or the spark of pride in your child's eye that moment when she at last gets long division.

Our children grow up when we're not looking. Days become years in the blink of an eye. To throw away even a single moment we've been given would be madness. So we learn to love the obligations. We find the good in bad plays. We appreciate the fashion forward design and bold color scheme of a uniform while watching an athletic sporting event. We even learn to love our Republican children despite their appalling politics. We dare not look away for fear of what we'll miss. We watch. We listen. And like our children, we hear everything and we commit it to memory.

SOMETIMES I'M FAT

I wake up in the morning, I look in the mirror. I get out of the shower, I look in the mirror. I stand up from my desk, I look in the mirror. I walk to my car after work, passing hundreds of reflective windows, I look in every mirror. *Maybe this time I won't look fat.*

I have struggled with my weight since I was ten years old. I remember back-to-school shopping and being forced to buy husky jeans. I remember those same big boy jeans not fitting. I remember as a teenager transitioning into the Big & Tall section, even though I was not tall. I remember alternating between loud prints and stripes because nothing is more slimming than looking like a circus tent. I remember over-sized blazers and layering layers. I remember believing the whole of the fashion industry existed to make me look as fat as possible.

As an adult I have cycled through at last a half-dozen different bodies. With my large frame I am never going to be "skinny", a fact that did not stop me from wasting away to a 32-inch waist in my early 20s. For good measure (and balance!) I later ballooned to a 48-inch waist in my mid-thirties. I have worn every shirt size, from a men's small to a gentlemen's XXXL.

Perhaps the worst part of my ever-changing body shape is that I never sync up with current trends. At my thinnest I was drowning in baggy jeans and over-sized sweaters in the mid-1990s. Low-rise jeans became all the rage around the time I started buying my pants from the tent and awning section. For a brief period my body was on-point and I was able to indulge in the skinny jeans movement. I shoehorned my meaty thighs and curvy ass into the skinniest low-rise I could find.

I am envious of every plus-sized gal I see. Women have so many options. They have entire stores dedicated to the fuller figure. They have foundation garments. They have beautiful women like Adele. But try being a fat gay man. Gay men have H&M with their impossibly tight t-shirts. Gay men consider crotch-hugging jeans a foundation garment. Gay men have that guy on *Modern Family*.

I have been at this for three quarters of my life. I don't know what the answer is...Diet? Exercise? Body acceptance? I have tried them all and they have all worked. And failed. My love-hate affair with fitness began when I discovered aerobics while attending college in the early 1990s. From the first grapevine I was hooked. My aerobic obsession eventually led me to the next level, step aerobics. In no time I was a full-blown junkie, attending class four to five times a week, the siren-call of Blue Swede's *Hooked on a Feeling* my theme song.

When I first started aerobics I was fat. I was fat and I was angry about being fat. That anger, coupled with a desire to finally lose my virginity, kept me coming back. With each kick, each twist, each punch, I was visually beating my fat into submission. I remember thinking: *If I keep doing this —* (grapevine, left) *— then maybe I won't be so fat —* (knee up, kick!) *— and then —* (gasping for air; step, ball, change) *— maybe someone will have sex with me.* Eventually I ooga-chaka'd my way from 230 pounds to 170 pounds, at long last achieving the kind of body that I assumed would help get me laid.

My love affair with aerobics faded after I left college. Our break-up sent me back to my first love, food, a disastrous rebound that lasted for more than a decade until a friend suggested I try yoga. I lost over eighty pounds doing yoga. But more than the weight loss, it was the mental clarity which I valued most. While my fellow classmates were namaste-ing their way to a peaceful Zen happiness, I was using the time to mentally stage fully-scripted revenge scenarios starring a revolving door of ex-boyfriends and that pushy woman from the grocery store. To be clear, it's not as if I would ever put these vengeful thoughts into action. I was simply allowing them to stop by for coffee and a quick chat before I returned to the business of living in the real world. I would leave each class feeling peaceful because rather than swallowing my rage I allowed it to have a voice.

Over the years I have come to realize that no matter how not fat I may want to be the real reason I exercise is to feel good about myself. It turns out all of those grapevines and crunches and half-assed attempts at camel pose had nothing to do with my desire to be physically healthy and everything to do with my need to be mentally healthy; now that I have kids that responsibility to maintain my inner garden is even greater. My children deserve to have the best version of me and that version cannot be irrationally angry or compulsively narcissistic.

I grew up feeling like an outsider, a stranger in a strange land. I never quite fit in and while my parents loved and supported me I'm not sure they knew exactly what to do with me. For the most part I was free to be myself. Left to my own devices and without much-needed guidance I struggled with being different. I stumbled awkwardly in adolescence, navigating an often unsuccessful path through my weirdness.

I would eventually learn to embrace and celebrate that same weirdness I now see in Chris. But unlike me at his age, Chris does not stumble or struggle. He happily marches to the beat of a different drummer. In fact, he is that drummer and it doesn't matter if he's the only one who can hear the music. Everyone else is just missing out. Some days I think I need to intervene and point him in the direction of the herd. Life will be easier for him, I tell myself. But of course that's not true.

When I was Chris's age my well-meaning father gently forced me into playing baseball. I imagine he did this because he thought he was making life easier for me. He wasn't and I hated it. Baseball was for boys who liked playing sports on a Saturday afternoon. I was not a boy who liked playing sports on a Saturday afternoon. I would rather have been at home playing with my sister's dolls. I resented baseball and over time I resented my father for making me play it. I was never any good at baseball, but still my Dad praised me and my "natural ability". He would tell anyone

within earshot that I had a stance like Pete Rose, leaving off
the part about how I threw like a girl (and I say that in the
context of the 20th century when such demeaning, sexist,
ant-feminist malarkey was still acceptable).

Now that I'm a parent I understand the reasons behind
my father's little white lies and subtle omissions. They were
designed to make me feel better, to balance out my weirdness
with some much-needed self-confidence. But is it okay to
lie? It's a dilemma I face every day with Chris and Elijah.
Chris takes piano lessons and he plays really well. I tell him
this every chance I get because it's true and I want him to
feel confident in his ability to play. He has also begun to
cook, simple things like omelets and cookies. When I ooh
and aah over a plate of his fresh-baked chocolate chip
cookies, I do it not just because I really like chocolate chip
cookies, I do it because he makes really good chocolate chip
cookies. I keep it simple. I tell Elijah he's smart because he is
smart. I hang up his artwork in my office because it's really
well done. I laugh at his silly jokes because they're funny.

But then there are those things the boys don't do very
well. Do I lie to them and risk having them grow up with an
unrealistic sense of their abilities or do I tell them the truth
and potentially crush their dreams? I struggle a lot with that
particular challenge. I don't want them to be that tone deaf

guy on *American Idol* who becomes the butt of a national joke, but if hitting those high notes, however poorly, brings them joy then who am I to stop them.

Ultimately I just want my children to have better self-esteem than I did. I don't want them to follow in my footsteps, rebounding from donuts to diets and obsessively checking every mirror to see if they look fat. I want them to move past the extra twenty pounds. I want them to abandon their revenge fantasies. I want them to do better than me because no parent gets it right every time. If our children can appreciate our faults then maybe they won't notice the mirrors.

THAT'S WHAT FRIENDS ARE FOR

And then we had to get married. We were technically married, in the eyes of the church, if not the law. Our first wedding took place in 2012, a full two and a half years before the legislative gods in Pennsylvania saw the progressive light. We were married in an actual church by an actual minister. It was all on the level with blessings and prayers and cake. So when it finally became legal for the gays in Pennsylvania to say *I do*, Todd and I were like, "Been there, done that."

It was great that we could now jointly file federal tax returns and visit each other in jail and make all sorts of next-of-kin end-of-life decisions, but for our money, we were married on February 18, 2012, no matter what the legislature said.

When we adopted Chris our marital status was irrelevant; we weren't required by the state of Oregon to be married. A few months after his adoption was finalized we received Chris's new birth certificate in the mail. It listed both of our names as parents. Elijah's adoption would be different. If we wanted both of our names to appear on his birth certificate the state of West Virginia required that we be married. Apparently it's only kosher for unmarried parents to be listed on a birth certificate when they're heterosexual.

I didn't mind this wedding 2.0. I could play along, dot the i's and cross the t's. I could even pretend to be a virgin a ~~third~~ second time. We were (re)married on February 7, 2015. A dear friend (and minister, natch) married us. The five-minute ceremony took place along the riverbank during a family trip to the science center. Elijah and Chris served as our best men. After the *I dos* we went back into the science center and had lunch. It was definitely a contrast to our big gay wedding in 2012. No guests, no heartfelt vows, no music. But we did have our children and that made up for everything, even the lack of cake.

Todd and I used to be social people. We used to host parties. We used to have a lot of friends. But that was before we had kids. Children consume your life and without even realizing it years have passed and the people you used to see every week are now strangers. I look back to our 2012 wedding and I remember all the people; a thoughtfully chosen small army of select family and our closest friends. People of a specific time and place, people we no longer see now that we have children.

I feel bad for no longer seeing these people. I admonish myself for not being a better friend, for not working harder to keep the relationship alive. I tell myself that all the other parents out there still see their friends every day, still host big parties, still stay out until midnight òn a school night eating chicken wings and singing karaoke at the local bar.

Of course, that isn't true. The other parents are just like us, trying to raise children as best we can, negotiating our new lives while juggling impossible schedules. We want to nurture these neglected friendships but life gets in the way. We intend to make time for lunches, grab a drink, send a text, but we don't. Life goes on, for us and them.

In the end, some friendships go the distance while others are of a moment.

I have had more than a few epiphany moments since becoming a parent two years ago. Chief among them was the realization that my friendships were no longer just about me. The company I was choosing to keep also affected my children. And some of my choices had been lacking. The people I surrounded myself with needed to be, if not role models, at least trustworthy. So I took an inventory.

My first stop was the internet. I knew that I would be littering the pages of social media with personal stories and photos of my children. In the weeks leading up to Chris's arrival I deleted half my Facebook friend list. Most of my erasures were no-brainers: the girl I once directed in a play but hadn't seen for three years; that homophobic guy from high school who I wouldn't remember if he came up to me and said, "Hey, I'm that homophobic guy from high school you don't remember"; the seldom-seem cousin with the appalling politics; people who use the acronym YOLO (as in, *You Only Live Once*).

Of course in the real word, that ever-shrinking dimension where face-to-face interpersonal communication still exists, ending a friendship is not as simple as clicking a button. It's one thing to erase a person in cyberspace, it's another thing to do so in the real world. And ultimately I was not going to cater to adult children when I had actual *children* children who needed me.

My inventory continued.

There was Peter Pan. The "every-other-word-is-fuck" guy. The slutty one. The emotional vampire. The passive aggressive narcissist. The lunatic. *What was I thinking?* At one time it had been cute. Their unwillingness to grow up. Their foul mouth. Their neediness. Their dangerous mental instability. Their overt sexuality so in your face at times you felt like their gynecologist. But what had once seemed colorful now seemed the opposite of where I was in my life.

Friendships are complex. Friendship is encouragement with caution. Faith with doubt. Laughter with tears. Friendship is being told those jeans make you look fat. It is giving while expecting nothing in return, but secretly kind of hoping you at least get a free Starbucks out of it. Friendships require work, but are not in themselves work. True friendships are rare. True friends, even rarer.

My once great circle of friends is a now a short line. It is a queue of the best people I know. In the absence of family we turn to these friends. A patchwork of aunts and uncles stitched together to make up for those missing who were accidents of birth. We trust these people to influence our children. Friends like Tom who taught my oldest son to embrace his inner theater diva during an eight hour car ride to Chicago, not stopping until Chris had perfected his one line, *Chicago! Chicago! It's a helluva town!* Friends like Jackie who acts as the perfect maternal foil to Elijah's paternal upbringing, prompting him to say, "If I had a mom, I'd want her to be you." And friends like Tyler who Chris looks to as the big brother he so desperately wishes he had, the ultimate role model.

We celebrate these friendships that have endured and we mourn the loss of those that did not. Some days I miss those lost friendships. I miss the inappropriate language and the insanity and closing down the bar. I miss the complexities of grown-up adult relationships. But then I look at the boys and a single smile makes up for a thousand nights of lost karaoke. For the first seven years of Chris's life we were strangers. Elijah has been with us for less than a year. There is a world to discover and I don't want to miss a minute when I have already missed so many.

BE CAREFUL WHAT YOU GOOGLE

The day we brought Chris home from Oregon I had one thought and one thought only: I need to delete the browser history on the computer. I briefly considered throwing away our old desktop and starting fresh with a new updated porn-free model, but that sounded expensive so instead I hit the delete button and introduced myself to the incognito window.

The internet changed the world. It connected us in ways we never imagined. It introduced us to a virtual world of infinite knowledge. It gave us YouTube celebrities and cat videos. It killed the encyclopedia. I love the internet. I spend hours each day ~~watching cat videos~~ ~~looking at porn~~ ~~taking Buzzfeed quizzes~~ enriching my mind.

The internet also made adoption easier. With a few clicks of the mouse I was able to view adoption databases all over the country. I could look at photos of waiting Inuit children in Alaska and then read about a sibling group in Texas. I could connect with caseworkers who otherwise would have no idea I existed. Without the internet I doubt our information ever would have made it to Chris's caseworker in Oregon and then where would we be.

So I'm not going to talk smack about the internet, except I am.

Before you have children the internet is a limitless utopia, an adult playground where anything and everything is possible. But after you have kids the internet is basically an unexploded grenade in the shape of big chocolate candy bar with a sign on it that says *Don't Eat Me*.

Every time Chris asks if he can go on the internet I experience what I imagine a stroke must feel like. My right arm goes numb, a sharp pain shoots through my brain, I forget how to breathe, everything goes dark and then twenty minutes later I wake up in a puddle of urine wearing my mother-in-law's wedding dress. Chris once asked me if we could Google pictures of bears. Five seconds later the screen was flooded with images of hairy middle-aged men. A few months later when he asked if he could see a photo of a baby inside the womb I thought it would be educational. But here's the thing: if you Google *baby in the womb* you still get the beaver shot.

I learned my lesson by the time we got to Elijah. He loves to say the word wiener. It makes him laugh. He calls me a wiener, he calls Chris a wiener, he calls his wiener a wiener. Elijah said Todd lived in Wienertown (he wishes!) and when Chris wondered if there was an actual place called Wienertown, Elijah suggested we look online. I don't think so, I thought. (For the record, I could not find a town named Wienertown. I did however discover that Wienertown is urban slang meaning "sausage fest; a place with a lot of men, particularly homosexual men.)

We finally gave in and allowed Chris to have email. We set up the account, including the password, and told Chris we would be monitoring it and periodically reading the correspondence. For the first few days he would just email Todd and me. *How are you?* I'm fine. *Can I play Minecraft?* No. *What are you doing?* Sitting next to you.

Eventually he started communicating with his classmates. We checked in with him and the messages were benign. Everything seemed to be going well. I was proud of the way Chris was handling this new responsibility. And then the school called. Unbeknownst to us, he and a boy in his class had been on video chat the night before. During the chat, they had dared one another to take off their shirts. The back-and-forth dares escalated from there. Chris told a teacher about the incident the next day at school and now the teacher was calling to tell me.

We should have been more vigilant. We had been naïve and we hadn't provided enough supervision. We deleted the account and the school had Chris and the other boy watch a video on internet safety. Of course it's impossible for us to continue the internet ban forever. Eventually he will need it for school or he will seek it out on his own accord or he'll turn 16 and realize we can't control his every move. One way or another he will find the internet.

We worry about internet predators. We worry about our children being exposed to inappropriate materials or sexually explicit websites. We worry that our best just won't be enough. We can set parental controls. We can restrict their access to devices. We can encourage them to make the best choices. Still, we can't watch them 24/7. We can't know what happens when they leave our four walls. As much as we might want, we can't force them to live inside a hermetically sealed bubble.

One day the internet will introduce them to the past. It took me all of three minutes to find the boys' birth parents on social media. It was strange to see my children's eyes staring back at me from the faces of these strangers who had made them. Within the hour I had located siblings, grandparents, the whole family tree. All of these people I had never met who were connected to my children. I could read their tweets, see their Facebook posts, scroll through their photos on Instagram. And for $4.99 more I could access their criminal records.

It used to be that children were adopted and that was the end of it. The past was the past. Records were sealed. Old connections were severed. But now nothing is final. *The past lives in a search engine.* A record of every word and image catalogued in a virtual world of things best left in yesterday. It's not that I want to keep the past from my children, I just want them to be old enough to face it.

But what happens when the past finds them? Because it will. There are no more six degrees of separation. Social media has changed the rules of the game. We are both separated and connected by a single profile. One day the past will come knocking on our door in the form of an instant message or a friend request. It may be from a curious long-lost aunt or a well-meaning sibling. It may be from the ghost of a birth parent they never knew. There are rules, but the past may not respect the rules.

I cannot control the past. I cannot rewrite the past. I cannot edit out the parts I don't like. The past is unchangeable. The past is part of my children.

For now we use the internet to discover the good parts of their stories. Chris is Native American, a descendant of a small tribe in Northern California with less than 4000 living members. When he had questions about his heritage we turned to the internet to explore his ancestry. The answers gave him roots. And just as we had a story before him, he had a story before us.

For now there is no email, no Facebook, no unsupervised Google searches. For now my children are five and nine years old. For now we use the internet to check the weather in West Virginia and Oregon. For now we live in the present. The past will still be there tomorrow.

THE NAME GAME

I named my first dog Max. I was 22 years old and living in my first apartment when I adopted Max. He was six weeks old. Todd and I had only been dating a few weeks but Max was just as much his dog as he was mine. I don't know why I chose the name Max. He was just a Max from the moment I saw him. It made sense. It fit. Over the years we would call him different names: Maxie, Maximus, Maxi-Pad, Nurse Max. It didn't matter. He happily answered to them all.

A year after Max came into our lives, we adopted Fred. Fred was an eight week old basset hound. He had been a surprise for Todd who had never had a dog growing up but had always wanted one. Todd was an ironic fan of the *Fred Basset* cartoon strip so once we had the basset hound naming him Fred was inevitable. Over the years we would call him different names: Red Fred, Freddy, Baby Fred, The Baby.

And like his brother Max, it didn't matter. He would happily answer to them all.

Loyal Nurse Maxie and sleepy Red Fred passed away a few years ago. We now have two miniature daschunds named Frank and Sam, and a cat called Bob. (We like old men names.) Naming is a rite of passage. When we named our dogs (and cat) it sealed a bond between us and them. It staked a claim.

A name gives you an identity. It is the moment when you start being you. Expectant parents spend months poring over baby name books, desperately trying to find just the perfect name as if it will decide their child's future. Choose poorly and your child could end up being a stripper (Tawney) or fat (Bertha) or President of the Future Homosexuals of America (Percy).

Names are powerful.

When books fail, parents reach back into the past and borrow from some distant limb of the family tree, never mind the name they selected for their child was carried by a cheating misogynistic unrepentant alcoholic racist. Or worse, someone who enjoyed kicking puppies. Sometimes parents just get lazy and phone it in slapping a junior on the end of what is already there in a weak attempt to maintain some sort of familial continuity.

And then there are those parents who follow trends. I was born in the mid-1970s. I grew up believing there were only three names in the world for girls: Jennifer, Melissa and Michelle. There were also a few Amys and a couple of Jessicas, but I imagine their parents were just troublemakers. More recently it has become de rigueur to name girls after pop stars, major U.S. cities and even alcohol (I'm looking at you Bailey, Hennessy, and Jameson). Just imagine the future fallout of those trends. One day we will have nursing homes populated by 90 year old women named Brittany and Arianna. Nurses will be forced to confiscate contraband Viagra from would-be 80 year old lotharios named Jayden and Hunter. After-dinner bingo will be presided over by the saggy-titted trio of Dallas, Cheyenne and Madison. These popular names may sound unusual to the Jennifers and Michelles of the world, but in the future the citizens of *The United States brought to you by Pepsi Co. a subsidiary of Halliburton* will think nothing of it.

Birth parents are given months to prepare before their baby arrives. There is ample time for careful consideration yet still they make choices that are willfully obtuse, naming their children after food, directions, celebrities, children of celebrities. They become so reckless in their quest to be unique they name their child Unique. Children have to live with these names. They are for life.

The first horrible thing many birth parents do to their children is name them. Sir Messiah. Jamillionaire. Cashmere. Audacious. Unesty. Player. (These were actual names from real case files we received.)

When you adopt you are not afforded the privilege of naming your child. It has already been done for you. Adoptive parents do not get to be obtuse or reckless or lazy. If a birth parent names his child Sir Messiah, the adoptive parent (and child) has to live with it. You cannot change a child's name, well you could, but common sense (and failing that, protocol) says you should not especially if the child is old enough to already know his name. The name, however unappealing it may be to you, belongs to him. It is part of his identity. And besides, keeping the name Sir Messiah won't make him any less your son and changing it won't erase the past he had before you.

Changing first names may be taboo, but it is common and accepted for adoptive parents to change middle and last names. We debated at great length when it came to our children's middle and surnames. When Todd and I were married we kept our maiden (as it were) names, neither of us taking the other's name with both of us agreeing that hyphens were unnecessarily showy. It seemed strange that we would now choose to saddle our children with two surnames and force the business of hyphens upon them. There was the option to use just one of our names but which name would we use and how exactly would we go about making that particular *Sophie's Choice*? Roll the dice? Hold a lottery? Conduct an online poll? Let the kids choose for themselves?

As the first kid adopted Chris would set the standard. Whatever name decisions we made with him we decided we would continue down the line and into the future. Christopher O'Donnell-Collar sounded ridiculous. Christopher O'Donnell appealed to my vanity, but Christopher Collar had the potential to be a great stage name. I suggested that he be known simply as Christopher, like Madonna or Charo. But in the end we realized what we had known all along, the name he had was perfect. There was no reason to change it. It was a part of his past. It was connected to his Native American heritage. It was who he was the moment we saw him. It made sense.

We had now established a precedent. Going forward none of our children would share either of our last names. For some people this name business might have been an issue, but for us it was immaterial. We didn't need to carry on legacies or signify ownership. We are no less a family and

Chris is no less our son for the lack of a common surname. Our connection was and is stronger than a few letters.

If first names were off-limits and last names were to remain unchanged, Todd and I decided that middle names would be fair game. Chris had no attachment to his middle name; it had been a throwaway placeholder with no ascertainable significance. We wanted this new middle name to connect him to us. We considered our names, first and middle, but nothing worked. Every possible combination felt like what it was, a throwaway placeholder.

We were up against a wall. The clock was ticking. We needed to make a decision. It was getting closer to finalization and if there were going to be any name changes we needed to submit them to the lawyer yesterday. Panic-stricken I turned to the internet. I was out of ideas and if there was one thing I had learned from my years on social media it was that someone on Facebook always has the answer.

In the end it was a woman from my yoga class who suggested the name. *Connell*. It was perfect. An effortless mash-up of our last names. It was unique, but not reckless. It was thoughtful, but not obtuse. It went with everything. Connell. It was the best of both of us. Chris loved his shiny new moniker. He loved what the name symbolized and we loved that he would forever carry a part of us with him.

At one time we had considered using this new name for all our children, but Chris would have none of it. Connell was his name. It belonged to him. Any future kids would need to go back to the well; the well being either Facebook or that woman from my yoga class.

As we moved closer to the finalization date for Elijah's adoption we found ourselves once again playing the name game. Elijah came to us pre-packaged with two middle names. We learned from a caseworker that his grandmother, with whom he lived for a year, had referred to him by a middle name. Elijah was only two at the time and had no concrete memory of being called by this middle name. We felt confident that we could start fresh with a clean slate, but we also took inspiration from that slate before wiping it clean.

Elijah would still have two middle names, but these names would now connect him to us. Eric and Michael. *Eric-Michael.* Todd's middle name and my middle name, with a hyphen thrown in for just a dash of unnecessary showiness.

We spent months searching for Chris's name, but when we found it, it made sense. There was no question it was the name he was always meant to have. And just as his big brother before him, Elijah has found the name he was always meant to have. This new name rolls off the tongue. It makes sense. It fits.

HOW TO SURVIVE THE HOLIDAYS

For many Americans, myself included, the last two months of the year are a happy time of reckless abandon and excessive binge-eating. It all begins at approximately exactly 9:37 p.m. on Halloween when, shortly after putting the kids to bed, you begin to steal their Halloween candy. At first you show restraint, taking only the loose Tootsie Rolls at the bottom of the pail. But by the end of the first week you've moved on to a steady breakfast of snack-sized Kit Kats and mini-Twizzlers. A midnight raid early in week two takes out the last of the king-sized Milky Way bars and you know you've hit rock bottom when your oldest son asks what happened to his jumbo Reese's Cup and you suggest the dog ate it.

No sooner are you beginning to show signs of early onset diabetes when you abandon the candy and move on to a gluttonous carb-fueled Thanksgiving feast where you consume enough food to feed all the starving children in

China dating back to the 1950s when parents still said things like, "You eat that meatloaf. There are starving children in China." Your reward for all your hard-eating is a 72-hour turkey coma followed by four weeks of Christmas cookies for dinner. Your shame spiral then comes full circle when, moments after receiving your yearly visit from the ghost of Dick Clark, you wake up hugging the toilet, your face plastered with bits of pork gravy and sick.

I love the holidays. When I was growing up they always had a fantastic quality about them. As I grew older they lost that feeling; it seemed to fade with each passing year. But now that we have kids the holidays have reclaimed some of their lost magic. They've been reborn. Easter, Halloween, Christmas. Especially Christmas.

The day after Thanksgiving we drive an hour north of our home and we cut down the biggest Christmas tree we can find. After I make Todd drag the tree back to the car, we set course for the mall and our annual visit with Santa Claus. Five-year-old Elijah will be in the *Cult of Claus* for years to come, but Chris is now staring down the barrel of ten. At this point his belief in the artist formerly known as Kris Kringle is rooted less in childhood innocence and more in a fear of what might happen if he stops believing. The clock is ticking. Of course I hope Chris believes forever.

It's selfish really, wanting my son to stay in this perpetual state of holly jolly arrested development. But I miss believing in that magic and the reasoning goes if he still believes then maybe just possibly Santa Claus is real. And if he's real then maybe he really does live in the North Pole with his grandmotherly wife and his army of extras from *The Wizard of Oz*. And if the wife and the little people are real then so are the flying reindeer. And if he can make reindeer fly then circumnavigating the globe in one night is suddenly not so impossible. And if it's not impossible then it must be possible and Santa Claus is real.

This is all I want because if Santa is real then I'm a kid again and not a cynical and jaded adult. Like the man on the radio as we drove to visit Santa that last time. His commercial voice announced, "The holidays are a stressful time."

Chris interrupted, "Why are the holidays stressful?"

I started to list the reasons: money, family, low levels of serotonin that bring on S(easonal) A(ffective) D(isorder). Midway through my list I realized he wasn't asking a question, he was making a point. *There is no legitimate reason for the holidays to be stressful. It's Christmas. It's magic. It's Santa Claus. Stop making this complicated. Just believe. It's that simple.*

Of course not all holidays are simple.

It was Father's Day. This year would be our first with Elijah and only our second as parents. As we discovered that first year with Chris, Father's Day presents a set of unique challenges to the house with two dads. For most families it is the mother who plans the brunch menu and buys the *World's Best Dad* coffee mug, but when both of your parents sport full beards the responsibility of honoring the day falls upon the shoulders of the very individuals the day is meant to celebrate.

The day before our big day we loaded the boys into the minivan and drove the five miles from our house to the mall. The four of us walked through, Todd and I surreptitiously pointing out to each other the things we expected to unwrap twenty-four hours later. We did this not only to ensure that we got what we wanted, but also because the boys have terrible taste.

Eventually we separated. I steered Chris in the direction of Todd's selections while Elijah was handed the jacket I had coveted. The next morning might not be full of surprises, but on the plus side, neither of us would be assigned the unenviable task of returning a bag full of ill-fitting garments come Monday morning.

Next up on the Father's Day to-do-list were greeting cards. The boys are in the habit of making hand drawn cards for birthdays and holidays. They sit down at the dining room table, however reluctantly, with broken crayons, dried-out pots of paint, worn-down-to-the-nub colored pencils and boundless imagination to create a world rivaling that of *Hallmark*. And since it's true that all previous card making exercises had occurred under threat of torture, I saw no reason Father's Day should be the exception. Also, the last thing I wanted to do was spend ten dollars on an overpriced, forgettable pre-fab greeting card that I would essentially be giving to myself.

No, the boys would make us Father's Day cards.

Already I could hear their voices, *You want us to do what? But there's two of you and if we each make you both a card that's four cards.* (I'm giving Chris a lot of credit with the math. It's likely he would say, "But there's two of you and if we each make you a card that's 27 apples.) *This isn't fair. This is discrimination. You're only doing this because we have two dads! All the other kids have only one dad, if that. All the other kids **buy** their cards. This wouldn't be happening if we had a mom. I want a mom. Why do you hate us? This isn't fair. Can we play Minecraft?*

I considered my options. I could force them each to make one card per parent. Four cards total. There would be tears, threats, spilled pots of paint. My second option was to have them work together on a single card for each parent. Two cards total. There would still be a protest and maybe even a few tears, but no spilled paint. The third option was for each kid to create -- on his own -- a card for one parent. Still two cards total, but this time without the threat of forced cooperation. No tears, no dramatic declarations, nothing but smooth sailing.

I loved my card from Chris. He wrote me a poem and drew me a picture of clothes because he knows how much I love to shop. (I later learned his first card had featured a beer bottle with *Happy Father's Day* written across the top. That kid.) Todd was equally pleased with Elijah's card. It had a dinosaur on it. I'm tempted to read too much into the Todd-as-dinosaur motif, but Elijah is five and dinosaurs are cool when you're five years old.

Of course the trials and tribulations of a two-father household Father's Day pale in comparison next to the awkwardness of a motherless Mother's Day. Our first Mother's Day with Chris passed with little fanfare. We were focused on his impending adoption, which was set to be finalized in a few days. I may have made a special dessert or maybe we went to a restaurant. I know that we went through the motions of the day although I can't remember specifics. I do recall collectively agreeing that while girls were perfectly nice we weren't really missing out on anything in their absence.

As Mother's Day lorded (ladied?) over us this second year it threatened to swallow everything in its estrogen-fueled path. Unlike Chris, Elijah was coming from a home with an established maternal presence. He referred to his foster mother as "my mom". It had been only a few months since Elijah had been placed with us and his connection to "my mom" was fresh. As much as we hoped to honor that connection it was important that we establish new traditions.

A friend who is a single father suggested that we were missing out by not celebrating Mother's Day. The way he saw it we were acting as mother and father so why not celebrate both days and get twice the attention and twice the gifts. His suggestion was valid and the extra attention and gifts appealed to me as a gay man because if there are two things gay men love its being the center of attention and opening up packages.

I considered my materialism and narcissism. Todd and I may be both mother and father but Mother's Day is for mothers. This year there would be no Mother's Day. This year we would try something new. We spent the night before our motherless Mother's Day wrapping presents and making cards for the boys. Later as I walked up the stairs to bed I looked over at the banner we had hung above the mantel. Its message for the day was clear: *Best Kids in the World Day.* The next morning we ate chocolate chip waffles with ice cream and then spent the afternoon playing at the park.

We didn't need Mother's Day. We didn't need the whole outdated model. We were this year's family trying to live in last year's calendar. It didn't make sense so we threw out the calendar and we created new traditions. Like *Chrisversary.* Every year on May 21 we celebrate *Chrisversary*, the anniversary of the day Chris's adoption became final. We have cake and presents because if I had my way every day would have cake and presents. In the very near future we will celebrate the *Fifth of Elijah* or *Elijahween* or some other equally clever day named in honor of the finalization of Elijah's adoption. There will be banners and presents and cake. Lots of cake. Because we like cake.

THE LAST DAYS OF DISCO

From almost the first day Elijah came to live with us our morning routine was the same. I would drop off Chris at his bus stop, then I would drive Todd to his office, and then before going in to work I would take Elijah to the coffee shop and pass the time until his pre-school opened its doors. Having come from a very small town in rural West Virginia, going to a coffee shop seemed a great adventure to our newest addition. Every morning he would stroll about the coffeehouse as if he owned it, putting on a show for the regulars who only encouraged him with their laughter and smiles.

After choosing a seat, always by the window, we would settle in with our drinks and snacks, pausing from our respective distractions to make small talk and share smiles. Over the next four months I worked my way through several books and he polished off a few seasons of *SpongeBob* on my phone. The minutes ticked by slowly during those first few weeks as we both struggled to settle into our new lives, but in those final days it seemed as if we had no sooner sat down then it was time to part ways.

Our last morning at the coffee shop was the last Friday before the first day of summer vacation. As we walked from the car we played our last game of *Booby-Trap Sidewalk*. Inside he performed his last show for the coffeehouse patrons. We enjoyed our snacks and drinks as if it were any other morning. I read my book and he watched his show, both of us acting as if Monday would be no different. He looked at me and smiled. I froze the moment.

I'm not nostalgic, except now I am.

My son is just five years old and already he is growing up.

I try to freeze every moment before the present fades into the past.

I think back to those early days with Chris, and I struggle to remember that first summer with him. Fresh off the plane from Oregon and we were strangers. We spent every moment of those three months together. We had our own routines and rituals. Every day was a great adventure. We made small talk and shared smiles.

I froze moments, but two years later, it seems not enough.

When you adopt they make you read books and take classes on how to be a parent, but for all their information what the books and classes fail to tell you is that children grow up and moments slips away. One day the seven year old turns nine and the next day the five year old is graduating high school.

Life goes on.

The year I turned forty Todd and I celebrated our eighteenth anniversary. We had two children, ages five and nine. The year my parents turned forty they celebrated their twentieth anniversary. They had three children, ages eighteen, thirteen, and nine.

On the surface it appeared as if we shared a similar path, my parents and I. But I was thirty-eight the year my then-seven year old son arrived and a few weeks shy of forty the day we met our almost-but-not-quite five year old. My parents welcomed their first child before they could legally drink. At an age when I was staying out singing karaoke until 2 a.m. my parents were raising a hormonal teenager, a defiant seven year old, and a free-spirited toddler.

I don't know how they did it.

Growing up we struggled. With Reaganomics failing to trickle down and mills closing up all across the rust belt, my Dad was often out of work. My Mom found full-time employment at a local department store, working overtime in a position she held even years after my Dad had achieved long-term job security. We lived in a series of rented homes. We were frequent visitors to the food bank. We bought groceries with food stamps. There was no extra spending money and no family vacations. Even McDonald's was a luxury.

Of course at the time we never knew this because my parents made sure we always had the things we needed. We may have bought our clothes from the sale rack at the discount store and eaten an unusual amount of *Hamburger Helper*, but we did not want for anything. When I look back I don't remember the struggles. I remember the Christmas Santa Claus came to visit us at the rented farmhouse. I remember makeshift picnics on the living room floor at the house on Market Street. I remember elaborate home-style birthday parties on Buffalo Street.

It's easy to romanticize the past. I look back on those years and all I remember is the unconditional love. I see myself as a teenager and I recall being a carefree and confident idealist, not an awkward and overweight misfit. My twenties are not a decade of chaos, but a series of adventures and new beginnings. Looking back on my thirties there are no shades of gray; too recent to be the past, the truth of the last decade is black and white.

I said goodbye to my twenties while sitting in a bar in Hoboken, New Jersey. I was horrified to be turning thirty, certain that I had done nothing more than waste all those years. It didn't matter that I was the first person in my family to go to college or that I had spent a year studying abroad in England or that I had realized my lifelong dream of living in New York, I was a failure. It was not the best attitude to take into my thirties.

I'm not sure what it was that I was meant to have accomplished by the time I reached thirty. I never had any great career aspirations or the desire to be rich and famous or a need to leave an impression, except suddenly I did. I suppose I wanted those things I didn't have simply because I didn't have them and if I couldn't, or didn't, have them then I'd pass the time stewing in a soup of regret in some dimly lit bar.

There is nothing more self-defeating than regret. Regret is a constant reminder of bad choices. Regret is failing even when you succeed. Regret is yesterday and last week, but never right now. Regret is pointless. In my thirties I stopped having regret. In my thirties I finally realized that every choice, every experience, every everything had helped me to get to this very moment, now. Regret wasn't my enemy, regret was my friend.

If I could go back to that bar on the eve of my thirtieth birthday I would celebrate. I would realize that being an awkward teenager had laid the foundation to becoming a confident adult. I would understand that every wrong turn was a new beginning. I would raise a glass to leaving college one credit short of graduation because I had chosen a path which two months later led me to Todd. I would embrace every obstacle because without those obstacles I would not be who I am.

I could look back at my thirties and remember the bad times, of which there were many. I could get lost in a maze of ill-conceived friendships and toxic relationships. I could focus on the difficult years in my relationship with Todd. I could punish myself for time wasted. But those moments and those people led me to now. Without all of it the timing would have been wrong. They gave me my marriage and my house and my job and my friends. They gave me Chris and Elijah.

These last days of my thirties have been the best days of my life. It's hard to imagine that me at twenty-nine would appreciate me at thirty-nine. I don't think my former self would understand the joy of quiet nights at home surrounded by family. I suspect he would rather be in a bar slamming back his fourth glass of regret, wondering where it all went wrong. I won't judge him though. He made me the person I am today.

THE BEGINNING (OR, THE EPILOGUE)

On the day I turned forty I had the sudden realization that my life was very possibly more than half over. It was a sobering thought. One that woke me from a night of half sleeps and disjointed dreams. My life is very possibly more than half over. And now I am left with this thought early on a Sunday morning. It keeps me awake and the dogs know I'm awake because they have started to do the *Dance of the Full Bladder* on my full bladder. Todd, no longer snoring, graciously offers to take them outside and make coffee, leaving me alone to ponder my half life.

It's a good life. I've done a lot. I've made friends. I've made impressions. I've seen the world. I've kissed a girl. I've kissed a boy. I've had great romances and passionate affairs. I've fallen in love. I've been happy and I've been sad. I've known great disappointment and even greater joy. I've made mistakes. I've said I'm sorry. I've laughed. I've been a husband. I've been a father.

And that's what it's all about. It took me thirty-eight years to become a parent, and yet it seems my life did not begin until the day I first met my son. So maybe my life is half over, or maybe it's just beginning.

Either way it continues. For forty more years, hopefully at least. More living. More adventures. Starting now. Because I'm awake.

15645149R00072

Printed in Great Britain
by Amazon